JULY

AUGUST

SEPTEMBER

OCTOBER

NOVEMBER

DECEMBER

Written by Anne McKie.
Illustrated by Ken McKie.

Published by
GRANDREAMS LIMITED
Jadwin House, 205/211 Kentish Town Road,
London, NW5 2JU.

Printed in Czech Republic

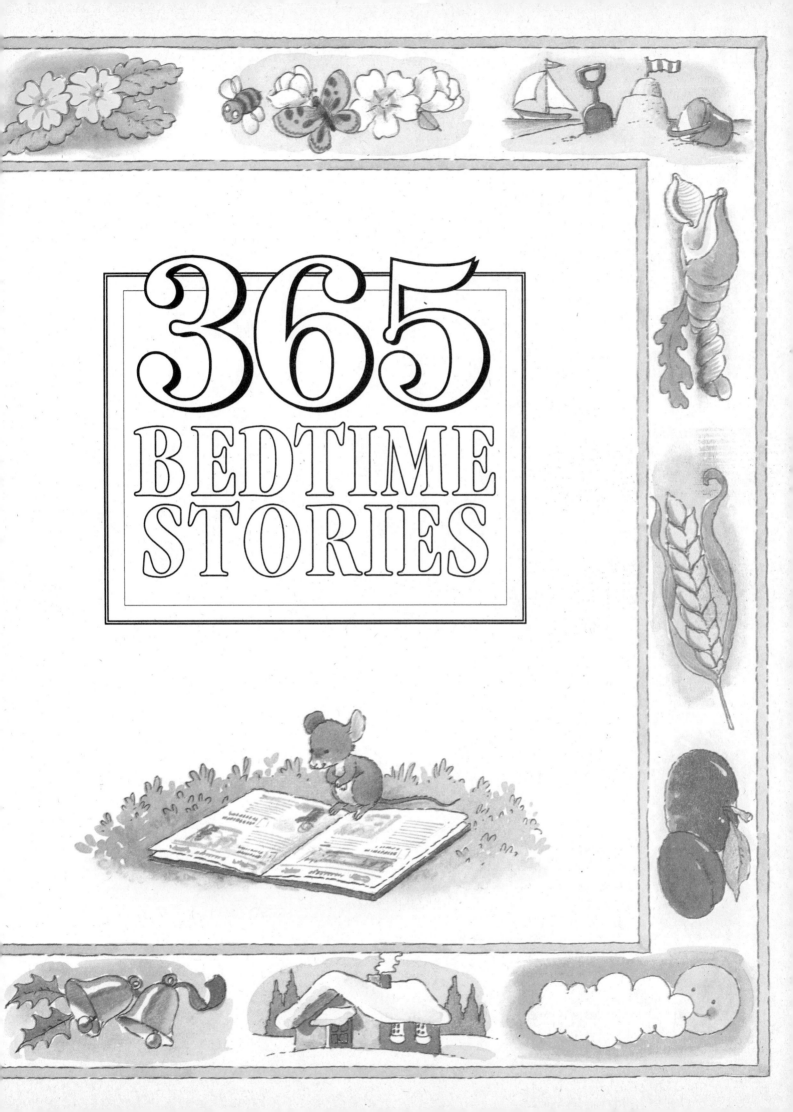

365 BEDTIME STORIES

A Brand New Year

It was the very first day of a brand new year and everyone had a holiday.

All the bears that lived on Big Bear Mountain were outside having fun in the snow. The whole day was perfect from beginning to end.

When at last it was time for bed, everyone agreed that it had been the best New Year's Day ever.

"I wish I could remember this day always!" said the smallest bear as he got ready for bed.

"That's easy!" Mother Bear smiled as she lifted him onto her knee.

"I've bought you a very special book. In it you write about all the things you have done each day. It's called a diary!"

So straight away everyone wrote on the first page of their diaries, and promised to fill it in every day for a whole year.

A Sweet Gift

In the New Year there are often lots of parties. Some families have parties before Christmas, during Christmas and in the New Year too!

Great Aunt Olive was very popular with her nephews and nieces, cousins and godchildren, and was asked to all their parties.

Now Great Aunt Olive had just one problem, she was running out of ideas for gifts to take.

"Don't bother to bring presents at all!" everyone told her, "Just bring yourself!" But Great Aunt Olive never liked to go empty-handed.

So every time Great Aunt Olive went to a party she made this special gift, and everyone agreed that it was the best present of all!

3 Dickie Makes A Mess

Dickie liked making models. He made them in plasticine, playdough and sometimes clay, and as his mother pointed out, he often made a mess!

One afternoon Dickie and his mother went shopping in a large store. "I'm going to buy you a special present," she told Dickie.

So straight away the little boy headed for the toy department, but his mother went across to kitchenware.

"Are you going to buy me some pots and pans?" Dickie asked. "I hope not!"

Then his mother picked up a large tray and chopping board. "Make your models on these, then no-one will mind how much mess you make!"

4 Lucille Is Late

Lucille the lop-eared rabbit was always late. She was late for buses, late for trains, she was even late for lunch.

"I don't mean to be late!" puffed poor Lucille when she arrived at last, quite out of breath.

So before she could be late one more time, her friends bought her a round silver watch she could pin on her dress.

Lucille was thrilled. Later that day she promised to meet them in the market, and can you believe it - she was one whole hour late!

"Why didn't you look at your new watch?" her friend asked.

Lucille gazed down at her shoes. "I forgot to mention, I can't tell the time!" Then she went very red indeed!

5 Lisa's Special Present

It was Lisa's birthday in a week. Now can you believe that this little girl couldn't think of a single thing she wanted as a present?

"There's nothing I really want," said Lisa, "I've got everything I need!"

At last the day of her birthday arrived and Lisa got lots of presents from her family and friends.

But none of them were for her! Instead there was a new lead and collar for her puppy, a basket and blanket for her kitten and toys for her hamster to play with!

6 Goodbye Christmas

Twelfth Night is the day that everyone takes down their Christmas decorations and packs them away until next year. It's time to say goodbye to Christmas.

"It was great trimming the tree and hanging up the decorations, but it's not much fun taking them down!" Ted moaned to his brother Toby .

"Everything looks so bare," Toby sighed, "and we're too short to reach some of the trimmings."

Just then the children's parrot Pedro landed on Toby's finger.

"Perhaps he wants to help!" laughed Ted. So Pedro flew up to the highest decorations and untied them with his sharp beak, and very soon everything was packed away.

"That wasn't so bad after all," said Ted to Toby, "Let's go outside and play now."

7

The School Pantomime

Paul and his brother Ben had parts in the school pantomime. It was called 'Jack And The Beanstalk'.

"We don't have to learn any words," they told their mum and dad, "but our part is secret!" Mum and Dad were puzzled.

The night of the performance arrived and the whole family came to watch Paul and Ben play their parts.

"Where on earth are they?" Mum whispered to Dad. "I don't see them on stage anywhere!"

The pantomime came to an end and all the audience clapped and cheered.

The boy who played Jack took an extra bow and so did Jack's mother. The giant who climbed the beanstalk came forward and so did the cow that was sold for beans. Then just before the curtain closed, Paul and Ben jumped out of the cow costume and bowed very low.

How the audience cheered, especially Paul and Ben's family!

8

Dilly's Crash Landing

Dilly Duck was flying high over the fields with her friends.

"Everything looks so beautiful in winter," quacked Dilly as she skimmed down low over the hedges. "I think I shall land on that pool down there and take a look around".

"Don't land there Dilly!" the others quacked, "or you'll be in for a surprise."

But Dilly took no notice, she was too busy showing off. "Watch me make a perfect landing everybody!"

What poor Dilly did not know was that the pond was frozen over. She skidded all over until at last she fell flat on the ice.

"Never mind!" gasped Dilly all the breath knocked out of her. "At least I've learned to skate!"

Bringing Home Logs

One day Danny woke up and looked out of his window. The snow was so deep that all the roads were blocked and the house was snowed in.

"We need extra logs from the woods," said his dad. "I'm afraid I won't be able to use my truck for some time!"

"I know what to do!" cried Danny and he showed his dad a picture in one of his books.

"Now that's a brilliant idea!" said Dad, and they went to fetch Danny's pony from the stable.

When they reached the woods, they made a sledge from branches. The pony pulled it along. A perfect way to get the logs home.

"The Indians first thought of the idea," said Danny as he rode his pony through the snow.

"What a good job you remembered it!" Dad laughed. "We'll be warm and cosy thanks to you!"

10 Jemima's Check Up

Joanne didn't want to go to hospital for a check up.

"There's no need to worry," her mother smiled, "no-one is going to hurt you and I'll be there all the time."

"I'll take my doll," said Joanne holding on tight to Jemima, "then I'll be fine!"

When Joanne was called into the doctor's room she was still clutching Jemima. The doctor looked across the table and nodded his head.

"I'd better take a look at this patient first," and he put his stethoscope on Jemima's chest and listened.

"Is she alright?" asked Joanne.

"Fit as a fiddle," laughed the doctor, "now let's have a look at you!"

When they got back home Joanne said to her mother, "I don't mind going to see the doctor again."

"No need!" laughed her mother, "you're fit as a fiddle too!"

11 Snowdrop The Magician

Mr. Magic had a rabbit called Snowdrop who helped him with his tricks.

Snowdrop enjoyed it when Mr. Magic pulled him out of his top hat and the audience clapped.

So one day Snowdrop thought he would perform some magic of his own. He reached inside Mr. Magic's top hat and pulled out a flag. Snowdrop pulled and kept on pulling until he was covered in strings and strings of flags.

The audience cheered so much that Mr. Magic let Snowdrop do his own tricks in the show.

12 Mr. Wolf Up To His Tricks

Mr. Wolf was always trying to trick the three pigs. "I will go and sweep the snow from their path," sniggered the wolf. "They will be so grateful, those silly pigs will open their door then I shall hop inside!"

So Mr. Wolf spent the whole morning clearing the snow from the three pigs' path.

"How very kind of Mr. Wolf!" said the three pigs as they watched through the window.

At last Mr. Wolf finished and hammered on the three pigs' front door. All of a sudden a great pile of snow fell from the roof and almost buried him.

"Many thanks!" cried the three pigs safe inside. As for Mr. Wolf, he went back home dripping wet with his tail frozen!

A Ride Home In The Snow 13

The weather was very bad, the school bus had to travel very slowly and all the children were late for school.

"I hope it doesn't snow too hard today," said the teacher, "or the bus won't get back through the snow, and you'll have to stay at school over night!"

The children didn't think much of that idea at all.

But all that morning it did snow very hard indeed, and in the afternoon the school bus wasn't able to pick up the children.

Not to worry! Look what's driving up to school instead...Farmer Turner and his sleigh!

How the children cheered. They'd rather go home on a sleigh than the school bus any day!

Lost In The Dark

One dark stormy night Mildred Mouse and her family were walking back home along one of the darkest paths. The wind was so strong it blew out all the candles in the tiny lanterns they were carrying to light their way.

"Oh my goodness!" cried Mildred. "It's so dark, I can't see a thing. I think we're lost!"

"No we're not!" cried one of the children. "I know where we are. We're standing right next to Grey Badger's back door. Shall I knock and see if he's inside?"

In no time at all, the mice were warming themselves in front of Grey Badger's fire.

"I had no idea the woodland paths were so dark at night," he said as the mice told him their plight. "Tomorrow I shall do something about it, I promise!"

So that night, Grey Badger guided Mildred and her family safely back home through the maze of tunnels that ran under the woodland, and it just so happened that one of them passed right next to Mildred's front door!

The Woodland Lights

At first light Grey Badger was up and busy! In one of his many cupboards he found strings of coloured lights left over from Christmas.

All day long he worked hard nailing up the lights on tree trunks all along the woodland paths.

That night when it grew dark, all the woodland animals came out to see their new streetlights.

"It looks like fairyland!" squeaked one of the young mice, clapping his paws with delight.

"How clever of you Grey Badger," said Mildred, but before she could thank him, Grey Badger had disappeared back into his burrow - he's rather shy you know!

16 One Cold Afternoon

Everyone who lived in Toy Village loved going outside to enjoy the cold weather. There was skating and skiing and everyone's favourite - throwing snowballs!

"This is wonderful!" called the china doll as she whirled around on her silver skates.

"Out of the way!" yelled the toy soldiers as they whizzed by on their bobsleigh.

The toys played out in the freezing weather all afternoon. Then, all of a sudden somebody asked, "Has anyone seen Ragdoll?" But no-one had!

"We must search for her at once," said one of the toy soldiers. "She may be lost or frozen in the snow!"

"Not me!" cried a familiar voice. It was the ragdoll, quite safe and sound.

"I hate the cold, so I've been in the warm kitchen all afternoon," she giggled. "I've made hot soup and roast potatoes to keep you all warm. So tuck in!"

17 Music By Dottie Dormouse

Dottie Dormouse loved music although she couldn't sing in tune and had never learned to play an instrument. In fact, she couldn't even whistle!

But in the middle of winter it was different. Dottie could play beautiful music!

When icicles formed on the branches outside her house, Dottie played such lovely tinkling tunes that everyone crowded round to listen.

Messenger Mole

18

Snow had fallen so thickly during the night that the woodland folk were finding it quite difficult to get around.

"I simply must get an urgent message to my sister," said Mrs. Grey Rabbit. "We could be snowed in for days!

Even the bigger animals like Fox and Grey Badger couldn't help, the snow was so deep.

"I could take your message for you!" piped up a tiny voice. It was a very small mole who had just popped out of his molehill.

"Now how can you possibly do that?" asked Fox bending over, "you're such a little fellow!"

"No problem!" said the small mole. "I could run through the secret mole tunnels that run underneath the woodland."

"So you could!" smiled Fox, "This snow could last for days."

"We'd all be very grateful," said Mrs. Grey Rabbit. "You can be our Messenger Mole."

The little mole blushed bright pink with pride and began delivering the animals' important messages straight away.

A Uniform For Mole

19

Miss Mole sat in her tiny underground kitchen in front of a warm fire. "If my nephew is going to deliver all these important messages, he'll need a special uniform."

So she rummaged in her sewing box and right at the bottom found a piece of shiny gold satin she had been saving to make a fancy blouse.

"I could put this to better use," she nodded and began sewing straight away.

What a surprise was waiting for Miss Mole's young nephew when he called later that day...A shining gold uniform with a special hat and a tiny mobile phone clipped to his belt!

"Messenger Mole at your service!" giggled the little mole. Then he gave Miss Mole a great big kiss to say thank you.

Freddie's Big Mistake

20

Freddie had lots of toy machines. He had trucks and tractors, lorries and diggers, he even had a toy snowplough.

Now one cold day he made up his mind to test out his toy snowplough in the snow.

"I wouldn't take your toys outside if I were you!" called Freddie's mother as she saw Freddie opening the back door. "You'll loose them in the snow!"

Freddie was quite disappointed, but very soon he came up with a bright idea. He would bring a bucket of snow inside and try out his snowplough on the kitchen floor.

At first the plough shifted the snow really well and Freddie was beginning to enjoy himself. Then bit by bit the pile of snow began to melt and water started to trickle across the kitchen floor.

Poor Freddie! He'll have plenty of mopping up to do when his mother finds out!

Stuck In The Snow

21

Next morning as Freddie's father was giving him a lift to school, he reversed his car out of the drive straight into a giant snowdrift!

"Don't worry!" said Freddie's father. "I think I hear something coming that can get us out of this mess!"

Sure enough a huge digger arrived to scoop up the snow from around the car.

Then a real snowplough cleared the road so Freddie could get to school.

22 Inquisitive Helen

Helen Hamster was very inquisitive. "I just need to know!" she would say as she poked her little pink nose into something else.

One day her mother was cooking in the kitchen. She lifted a pan off the stove and put it down safely on the table.

"On no account lift the lid Helen!" she warned as she left the room.

Now that was too much for Helen the inquisitive hamster. She tiptoed towards the table and very very carefully lifted the lid just the tiniest bit...POP! POP! POP! POPCORN!!!

It shot out of the pan and whizzed round the room like firecrackers - very soon Helen was covered in it!

Now you may think that this cured Helen of being inquisitive. Not for a minute - but that's another story!

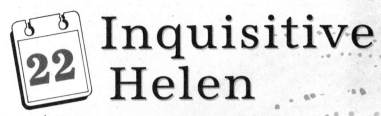

23 Tasha The Dachshund

Tasha the dachshund hated cold weather. He didn't like going outside in the snow and getting his feet wet and his tummy frozen.

"Please come out and play," pleaded Jennie his young owner, but Tasha pretended that he was fast asleep on the rug by the fire.

Now Jennie really wanted Tasha to come outside and have some fun, so she found her skipping rope and her mother's biggest tin tray, then she squeezed Tasha into his tartan jacket and carried him outside.

"Now isn't this fun?" Jennie asked her little dog as they went down the street.

"I think it's very embarrassing," mumbled Tasha to himself, "and I hope nobody sees me!"

24 The Indoor Garden

Little Miss Potter had to stay indoors. It was very cold and the paths were far too slippery for her to go outside because she is a very old lady.

"I shall miss my garden for a while," said little Miss Potter sadly. "I shall have to look out of the window instead."

She needn't have worried. The two children from the house next door made her a miniature garden of her very own, from an old dish filled with bulbs, twigs and moss.

"This is just what I want," said little Miss Potter as she thanked the children. "I shall enjoy my indoor garden until the spring comes."

25 Sheila's Sweater

"When are you going to wear the new sweater Grandma knitted for your Christmas present?" Sheila's mother asked her.

"Grandma must have used the wrong measurements!" Sheila sighed as she pulled it on. "It's so long it almost reaches my ankles!"

Just then, Sheila's mischievious kitten Flossie pulled and pulled, the sweater began to unravel.

"Now it's a perfect fit, thanks to Flossie!" said Sheila with a grin.

26 A Visit From Jack Frost

"I wonder if Jack Frost has been?" said Sue's mother as she opened the bedroom curtains on a freezing winter morning.

"Who is Jack Frost?" asked Sue. "Is that the postman's name or is it the milkman?"

Sue's mother laughed. "Wait and see!"

Now one cold morning when the temperature fell well below freezing, Sue's mother opened the bedroom curtains and said, "You've had a visit from Jack Frost at last. He's been in the night and painted all those lovely patterns on your window!"

It was Sue's turn to laugh. "I thought Jack Frost was a real person, not just the cold winter weather!"

27 Mr. Wolf Gets A Shock!

The three little pigs lived together in a new house built of bricks. However hard Mr. Wolf huffed and puffed, he could never ever blow it down!

All the little pigs were warm and safe inside when the north wind blew in the winter and that was the time Mr. Wolf went out hunting for a tasty meal.

The three little pigs knew he had been creeping round and round their brick house because they found his great paw prints in the snow. So very early one morning, they set to work to shovel all the snow they could find into a huge pile.

"Is that old Mr. Wolf in for a shock when he comes round the corner!" squealed the three little pigs.

He certainly was! When he saw the terrible snow monster the pigs had made, he ran back home, locked his door and never came out again until spring!

Knitting Norah

28

The zoo keeper's wife Norah always helped with the animals. She cut and minced up their food and always knew exactly what they wanted. She took their temperature when they felt ill, and gave them nice medicine to help them feel better. She was a very busy lady!

Now when Norah had a bit of spare time, which wasn't very often, she would reach into her sewing cupboard and get out her wool and knitting needles.

Norah knitted all sorts of things - gloves for the gorillas, muffs for the monkeys, she even knitted teeny weeny socks for the scorpions!

Now during a spell of very cold weather the zoo keeper asked Norah a special favour. "It will use up all the wool in your sewing cupboard and take ages and ages!"

So Norah set to work and after eight long evenings she had knitted the longest, stripiest scarf you have ever seen.

Can you guess who it was for?

Pins And Needles

29

When the other insects and creepy crawly things saw the scorpions' socks they all had the sulks!

"I would love a woolly sweater!" sighed the slimy slug. The green grasshopper wanted white socks (two pairs of course). The ladybird asked for a hat and the snails begged for headbands.

"Stop!" cried the zoo keeper, "These things are far too small to be knitted at all!"

But Norah knew better. In just one evening she had finished and everything fitted perfectly. Do you know why? She had knitted on pins instead of knitting needles!

The Blizzard

30

"What's a blizzard?" Chris asked his sister Mo one cold winter's day.

"I think it's an animal with scaly skin and a scraggy neck!" said Mo, who had no idea at all.

"No it's not!" yelled Chris, who was feeling bored, and he threw a cushion across the room.

Mo picked it up and threw it back, and in no time at all the two children were having a cushion fight.

All of a sudden the cushion burst and hundreds of feathers flew all over the room.

"It's just like a blizzard in here!" shouted their mother angrily as she flung open the door. "You two are going to have some cleaning up to do!"

Edward To The Rescue

31

Edward the elephant was standing on the airstrip polishing his plane.

"I don't think I'll go up today," he said out loud. "There's a thunderstorm coming!"

Just then the radio in his plane crackled, 'Severe weather warning, cyclone approaching, no flying today!'

When Edward heard the radio message he gasped because he had just seen some of the bigger birds flying over the airfield. "They're taking part in the Flamingo Cup Race today, and they won't have heard the weather warning!"

In next to no time, Edward had jumped into his plane and was flying towards the birds. He flew above them and shouted down, "Perch on my wings and I'll fly you safely back home."

The birds were very grateful to be back on the ground. By the time the storm arrived they were safe indoors thanks to Edward the flying elephant.

1 Mr. Magic And The Chef's Hat

One afternoon, Mr. Magic arrived at a party without his top hat.

"Whatever shall I do?" he asked his rabbit Snowdrop. "I can't do any conjuring tricks without my top hat!"

Quickly Snowdrop hopped off to see what he could find.

Very soon he came back with a big white tall hat - it belonged to the chef in the kitchen.

Then Mr. Magic began pulling all sorts of delicious food out of the hat, even the chef was surprised - he could sit back and enjoy the party!

2 Reggie Rabbit Scares Mr. Fox

Reggie Rabbit liked to draw. He always carried a pocket full of pens and pencils.

One day when Mr. Fox was out jogging, Reggie crept into his house through the bathroom window. He took out his black pen, and what do you think he drew? A big black hairy spider in Mr. Fox's bath! Then Reggie hid outside until Mr. Fox returned.

"I can't wait to get into a lovely hot bath!" puffed Mr. Fox as he jogged by.

Reggie didn't have to wait very long before Mr. Fox's front door burst open. "There's a big black spider in my bath," he screamed. "Help anybody! Help! Help! Help!"

3 Sophie's Boots

The snow was melting and the roads were wet and muddy. Little Sophie's mum took her to the shops and bought her a pair of wellington boots.

Now Sophie had never had a pair of boots before and she was very proud of them.

"Would you like to jump in puddles and splash about in your new boots?" asked her mum.

But Sophie shook her head and stayed inside instead. She couldn't bear to get her new boots dirty!

That night when Sophie's mum went into her room, she found the little girl fast asleep in bed - still wearing her brand new wellington boots!

4 The Wooden Spoons' Party

"It's very crowded in this kitchen drawer," said one of the Wooden Spoon people.

"Move over a bit," said another, "I'm squashed!"

Now when the Wooden Spoon people looked more closely, they found that their kitchen drawer was full of paper hats and balloons - in fact all the things you need for a party.

"Let's have a party tonight when the rest of the house is asleep!" cried some of the spoons. And so they did, but they made quite sure to put everything back in its right place, before the family got up the next morning.

The Missing Lamb

5

It was a bitterly cold day. The north wind was blowing and the farmyard was covered with snow.

"I can't find one of my newborn lambs," said the farmer, very worried. "I've searched everywhere!"

"Don't worry!" laughed the farmer's wife. "Your little lamb knows where it is warm and cosy. She has trotted into the farmhouse and settled down next to the kitchen stove!"

The Pig With Good Manners

6

"It is most important to have good manners!" Polly the pig told all the animals in the farmyard.

"I always sit up straight. I never push and shove. I don't yell or shout and I never ever say rude words!" said Polly, and she stuck her nose up in the air.

"That is quite true," replied the farmer's wife. "Polly has perfect manners, until I say DINNER TIME!"

Now look at Polly! She puts her feet on the table. She grabs all the food and gobbles it up, but worst of all, she eats with her mouth open and makes a dreadful noise!

Where are all your good manners now, Polly?

7 Fun In A Puddle

It had been raining all day and Minnie and Winnie were very bored. They had done all their jigsaws, read all their storybooks and played with all their toys.

"What would you really like to do?" Minnie asked Winnie.

"I would like to go outside and play with the biggest puddle we can find!"

"Then let's do it!" cried Winnie. So they both went outside in the rain and had a marvellous time.

8 Grandma's Presents

Dolly, Molly and Holly had spent all their pocket money.

"Have you forgotten Grandma's birthday in a couple of days?" asked their mother.

The three girls gasped. "What are we going to do?" they all cried.

"How about making your Grandma something?" suggested Mother. "She would probably like that better than a bought gift."

So the three girls set to work. Dolly chose shells, Molly chose stones and Holly chose pine cones.

On her birthday, Grandma was thrilled. "Much better than bought presents!" she said, her face beaming.

She put Dolly, Molly and Holly's presents on her mantlepiece where she could look at them all the time.

9 Uncle Wills Carves A Cradle

Uncle Wills made things from wood, and when Jill's little sister was born, he promised to make her a cradle. He started straight away, cutting and shaping and carving the wood.

Now Uncle Wills always made a splendid job of what he did, but he was very very slow!

Weeks went by and Uncle Wills was busy carving the cradle. Months went by and Jill's baby sister grew bigger. Years went by and Uncle Wills was still carving but Jill's baby sister wasn't a baby any more!

One day she came to see Uncle Wills. When she saw the beautifully carved cradle, she was delighted. "What a perfect bed for my dolls!" she cried. "Please may I have it, Uncle Wills?"

10 Willy's Worm

One day Willy the worm poked his head through the soil and a very strange sight met his eyes.

"Another worm!" cried Willy very excited. "But what a strange looking fellow!" and Willy wriggled across to meet him.

"Aren't I a silly Willy!" he said blushing. "It's only a shoelace!"

11 Otto To The Rescue

Mrs. Grey Rabbit told her children that they should always use the stepping stones when they wanted to cross the stream. "Be very careful to look where you are going and don't be in a hurry!" she told them again and again.

But the youngest rabbit didn't listen. He hopped and skipped from stone to stone, whistling and singing and gazing up at the sky. Halfway across, he missed his footing and fell into the water with a loud splash!

"Help, somebody help!" he squealed. "I can't swim!"

Luckily, Otto the otter, whose home was close by in the roots of an old willow tree, heard the little rabbit's cries.

Otto slipped swiftly into the water and rescued the little rabbit in next to no time.

Mrs. Grey Rabbit was so grateful she said that Otto should have a medal, but instead she gave him a big kiss!

12 Badger's Bright Idea

Next morning Mr. Grey Badger went to see Otto.

"These stepping stones across the stream are getting very dangerous," he told Otto. "I could build a wooden handrail, but I shall need some help to fix the posts into the bed of the stream."

"What are we waiting for?" asked Otto, and he grabbed a hammer and nails, and dived into the water.

After a lot of hard work, the handrail was ready.

"Let's ask the grey rabbits to be the first to try it," suggested Badger.

"And I'll be here to rescue them if they fall in!" chuckled Otto.

13 Pop-up Toast

Every morning the crocodile and the alligator woke up bright and early.

The crocodile made a big pot of fresh coffee and the alligator made the toast.

"Can we swap over one morning?" asked the crocodile, "and I'll make the toast for a change."

"Not likely!" snapped the alligator as he bit into his twelfth piece of hot toast.

"It's perfect the way it is!"

14 A Valentine For Mole

It was Valentine's Day and Messenger Mole was busy from morning to night.

Everybody in the woodland had sent gifts and cards to their sweethearts. The rabbits had sent red roses to each other. The fieldmice had sent heart-shaped boxes of chocolates, and Mr. Fox had sent Mrs. Fox a huge bottle of Foxglove perfume - Messenger Mole could hardly carry it!

At last every card and present was delivered and Messenger Mole set off for home.

As he opened his front door, he got quite a surprise. His little house was full of Valentine cards and gifts for him.

"I must have lots of secret admirers!" giggled Messenger Mole going very red!

15 Tessa's Truck

As the snow melted, it left big muddy puddles all over the farmyard. When the farmer drove the tractor through the gate one morning, the wheels got stuck fast in the soft mud.

"Can someone give me a push?" cried the farmer. "I can't stay here all day!"

Although the animals and the farmer's wife pushed very hard, the tractor wouldn't budge at all, so the farmer fetched Harvey the heavy horse from the stable.

Harvey pulled and pulled with all his might, but still the tractor stayed firmly stuck in the mud.

"I know what will shift it!" cried the farmer's wife, so straight away she sent for her friend Tessa from the garage.

Tessa came as quickly as she could, driving her brand new breakdown truck.

"I'll have you out in a jiffy!" shouted Tessa as she hooked the tractor up to the winch on the back of the truck.

"Well done!" everybody yelled as the tractor was pulled from the sticky mud.

"Three cheers for Tessa and her breakdown truck!"

16 The Popping Pea Pod

Five little spring onions were marching along in a line. How smart they looked, how straight and tall!

On they marched, left right, left right, in perfect time.

All of a sudden a pea pod went POP! and the spring onions almost jumped out of their skins.

17 A Kit For Ivor

Ivor had been given a present. "I've never had anything like this before," said Ivor as he opened the box. Inside were lots of pieces of metal, nuts and bolts, and all kinds of strange parts.

"It's a kit," said Ivor's dad. "You make it up yourself."

So Ivor read the instructions carefully and set to work.

"Do you need any help?" asked his dad after a while.

Straight away a strange voice answered, "No help needed!"

It wasn't Ivor, it was the robot he had built from the kit who answered!

I think Ivor is going to have a great time with his robot, don't you?

18 A New Member For Ivor's Family

Early next morning Ivor ran to the nursery to see his new friend. As he approached he heard strange tones, and not only those of the robot.

As Ivor opened the door, he couldn't believe his eyes. His robot had created a pet of his very own to play with - a puppy!

19 Ivor's Fantastic Machine

Ivor soon discovered that his robot could build anything.

He made Ivor the most fantastic machine you can imagine, it almost filled the bedroom.

"It's far too big to keep inside," said Ivor's mum.

She needn't have worried, in next to no time, Ivor's robot had taken the fantastic machine to pieces and assembled it again, outside in the garden.

20 The Robot's Toys

Sometimes when Ivor's robot had a bit of free time, he would search in Ivor's toy boxes for any spare parts - screws, wheels, bolts and gears - they all came in useful.

Then he would make things, just for himself. (But he does let Ivor play with them too!)

21 Spring-cleaning

Mrs. Grey Rabbit was busy with her spring-cleaning.

"This room needs decorating," she said as she gazed round at the grubby walls. "I shall ask Messenger Mole to take a message to Badger, he's very good at hanging wallpaper."

Now when Messenger Mole returned from Badger's house, he brought bad news. "Mr. Badger has a cold and can't come out today!"

"Not to worry!" cried the little rabbits. "Mother has gone to fetch some paint, so we'll start to hang the wallpaper straight away!"

When Messenger Mole saw the mess the little rabbits were making, he thought he should stay to help.

Now when Mrs. Grey Rabbit returned, she gasped with dismay. There was paper and paste everywhere - except on the walls!

"Everybody outside!" she cried. "No more spring-cleaning for today. We'll wait until Mr. Badger's cold is better before we do anymore!"

22 Busy Badger

The very next day Mr. Badger arrived at the rabbit's home. His cold had vanished and he felt fit enough to tackle anything.

In less time than it takes to tell, he had wallpapered the room.

"In my opinion it looks rather plain!" he told Mrs. Grey Rabbit as he looked around. So he gave the little rabbits some scissors and lots of different coloured paper.

Now look what a difference they have made. The little grey rabbits were quite helpful after all!

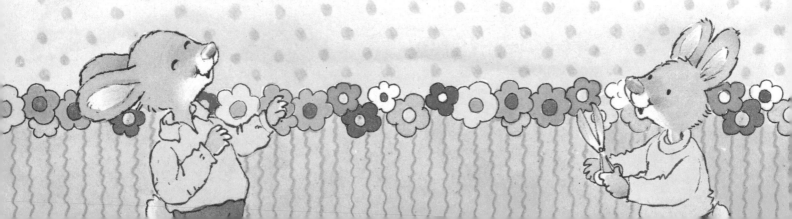

Harriet's Pile Of Books

23

Harriet's favourite place was the library. She could read quite well and loved choosing her own books to take home.

One day Harriet went into town with her mum. She visited a place with lots of books. Straight away Harriet chose a big pile of them to take home.

"Stop!" shrieked her mum as Harriet marched through the door holding onto her books. "You're not in the library now Harriet! This is a book shop and all those books have to be paid for!"

"Sorry!" giggled the little girl. "I'd better put them back at once!"

"Just choose one," smiled her mum. "We'll pay for that, then visit the library tomorrow!"

Harriet's Beanbag

24

"I need a new beanbag," Harriet told her mum. "Mine has a hole in it and the beans are spilling out all over the place!"

So off they went to buy a new one. Now on the way home, Harriet called in at the library. She took her new beanbag inside, and when she had chosen a book, she sat down on her beanbag to read.

Suddenly, the gentleman who looks after the library came over and saw Harriet sitting comfortably on her new beanbag.

"Now that's a good idea!" he said. "I'll buy lots of those, and all the children that visit the library can sit on beanbags and read!"

Mud Pies

25

When Ashley was looking in the shed, he found his bucket and spade that he had taken to the seaside last year.

"It's a long time before my summer holiday," sighed Ashley. "I think I shall take my bucket and spade outside and make pies!"

Just look at the weather. Ashley couldn't make sand pies, so he made mud pies instead!

26

Ashley's Muddy Shoes

Ashley's shoes were very dirty. As he walked home from school, he had jumped in every muddy puddle he could find.

"It's time you learnt to clean your own shoes!" said his mother when she saw the state of them.

"Leave them to me!" said Ashley cheerfully and began straight away.

"Haven't I made a good job of them?" grinned Ashley as he held up his gleaming clean shoes.

"You certainly have Ashley!" sighed his mother.

27 Kim's Fridge

"The snow is going at last," smiled Kim's mother. "Spring is coming, I can feel it!"

Kim looked out of the window. There was just a pile of snow left in the garden, and it was melting very quickly.

Later that day, when Kim's mother was making a meal, she opened the fridge door, and what do you think she found? A bowl of frozen snow!

"Just trying to make it last a bit longer," said Kim with a grin. "It's a long time till next winter!"

28 Pancakes For Mr. Wolf

The three little pigs were so busy in the kitchen, they didn't notice Mr. Wolf peeping through the door.

"Wonderful," whispered Mr. Wolf. "First I shall eat the three little pigs' pancakes, then I shall eat the three little pigs!"

"Can I toss the next pancake?" yelled one little pig as he grabbed the frying pan.

The big fat golden pancake flew high into the air, then landed with a plop, right on top of Mr. Wolf's head!

How he yelled and shouted as he ran down the garden path, because the pancake was very hot and sticky.

"Serves him right," cried the three little pigs. "Now let's make some more pancakes!"

1 ## Clarissa The Duck

Clarissa the duck was a great favourite with the farmer and his wife.

"Don't leave the farmyard," warned the farmer, "you might come to some harm!" And he picked her up and gently stroked her soft white feathers.

But Clarissa was a bit of a scatterbrain and soon forgot what the farmer had said.

"I shall put on my new spring bonnet and stroll over the bridge to see the daffodils in the wood," Clarissa quacked loudly as she marched through the farmyard gate.

Now who should be laying in wait behind the gatepost but Mr. Fox. "I'll follow this plump little duck and save her for my dinner with new potatoes and green peas!" he sniggered.

So off went Clarissa towards the wood without noticing Mr. Fox close behind her.

"The bridge over the stream looks very rickety," quacked Clarissa as she tiptoed across. But Mr. Fox didn't notice, he stepped onto the creaky old bridge and fell through with a great splash into the stream!

As for Clarissa, she had already crossed the bridge with care. She went into the wood to admire the daffodils, then she flew back to the farmyard without even noticing Mr. Fox at all!

2 Jed Solves A Problem

Jed's baby sister had a new doll. She liked it so much she wouldn't let it out of her sight. In fact, when Jed's baby sister couldn't see her new doll, she screamed and kept on screaming.

"This is going to be very difficult at meal times!" sighed Jed's mother.

So Jed fetched his old highchair, sat the doll inside and put it right next to his baby sister's chair. Then they could both sit up to the table!

3 Norah's Wash Day

The animals at the zoo kept Norah very busy. She was the zoo keeper's wife and loved and looked after the animals as well as the keeper, so all the animals liked to help her in return.

One very windy day Norah got up early to do her washing.

As she hung it out on the line to dry, she said to the animals, "In this wind my clothes will soon be dry, and when I have done my ironing, I shall spend the rest of the day with you."

But when Norah looked across at her washing hanging on the line - it was perfectly still! The strong wind had dropped and her clothes were dripping wet.

"It will take ages to dry!" sighed Norah.

"I don't think so," chuckled the zoo keeper as he pointed to the washing flapping wildly. Thanks to the elephants, Norah's washing was dry in no time!

Paul's Problem Trousers

4

Paul's trousers were always falling down. Bill laughed because his stayed in place all day long.

"You need a smaller size," said Paul's mother, and she bought him a new pair.

But Paul's trousers still fell down, which made Bill laugh even louder.

"You need a broader belt," said Paul's mother, and she bought him a brown one with a brass buckle.

But Paul's trousers still fell down, and Bill laughed until he cried.

So Paul's mother bought him a pair of the most wonderful braces. Paul's trousers never fell down again (thanks to the wonderful new braces) and Bill sulked because he wanted a pair!

Rachel's Lost Kitten

5

Rachel had a new kitten who loved to hide in the strangest of places.

She hid in the laundry basket. She hid round the back of the armchair. She even hid underneath the flowerpots. Rachel was always looking for her!

One day Rachel couldn't find her new kitten anywhere. She searched every room in the house, then she looked outside in the garden.

But no-one thought of asking the dog - he knew where Rachel's kitten was hiding all the time!

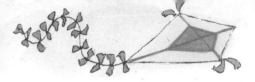

The Shy Little Kangaroo

6

One day some friends of the Shy Little Kangaroo called at his house and asked him to come out to play.

"Are you good at skipping?" asked Koala Bear.

"'Fraid not," whispered the Shy Little Kangaroo, "I get all tied up."

"Can you play cricket?" asked Cockatoo.

"I can't hit the ball," the Shy Little Kangaroo answered quietly, "but I can play hopscotch!"

And off he went leaping down the road to show them how.

Wesley Wombat

7

"Let's have a ride on the seesaw," said Wesley Wombat to his friends.

So everyone jumped on, but the seesaw didn't go up and it didn't go down.

Along came the Shy Little Kangaroo and he began to laugh. "You're supposed to sit on each side of the seesaw, then one side will go up, while the other side goes down. I'll show you how!" cried the Shy Little Kangaroo.

He jumped on the empty end and all the others flew up in the air!

8 Follow-my-leader

Dolly, Molly and Holly liked playing follow-my-leader. They played it on the way home from school, through the park and up the garden path. They played follow-my-leader through the back door and across the kitchen floor, where they made three sets of muddy footmarks.

"Right!" said their mother. "You can play follow-my-leader with a mop and bucket until my floor is clean once more!"

9 The Party Puppets

At Jane and Tim's party, all the children were looking for the puppet man.

"He's arrived!" cried Jane. "I can see his car in the drive."

But Bill, the puppet man, took ages before knocking at the door.

"I'm afraid I've forgotten my puppets!" he said looking dismayed. All the children seemed disappointed and one of them began to cry.

"Find some string and we'll be your puppets," laughed Jane and Tim.

Everyone cheered up at once, and the puppet man and his real puppets gave a wonderful show.

10 The Wrong Coat

Fizzy Grizzly went out to lunch. He drank lots and lots of his favourite fizzy drink, and ate one, two, three maybe four double hamburgers with cheese - but who's counting?

When he felt absolutely full up, he put on his coat and left for home.

Halfway down the road, Fizzy Grizzly put his hands in his pockets. Somehow I think Fizzy Grizzly has put on the wrong coat, don't you?

11 See And Be Seen

"On grey misty days," said Mrs. Grey Rabbit, "it is very hard to find my children when they are out playing in the wood."

"On rainy days everything looks grey, even us!" said one of the little rabbits. "No wonder our mother can't find us!"

Now just by chance, Mrs. Grey Rabbit happened to look inside her cupboard where she kept all sorts of useful bits and bobs.

On the very top shelf was a big roll of yellow material. It was almost too bright to look at!

Straight away Mrs. Grey Rabbit took out her sewing machine and was busy, busy, busy!

Soon every one of her little grey rabbits had an outfit of the brightest yellow.

"Now I'll be able to find you wherever you are!" smiled Mrs. Grey Rabbit, very pleased with her efforts.

12 Aunt Mary Moppit's Curtains

Aunt Mary Moppit bought some new velvet curtains for her window, but they were far too long.

"I shall have to cut a lot off the bottom!" said Mary as she took out her scissors.

"I'll have plenty of velvet for another pair of curtains," she laughed, "but I haven't another window!"

Then she looked at her car, her little dog and the rabbits in her garden and they gave her an idea.

She picked up the spare velvet and began to sew. "Now I have lots of soft toys to give to my young visitors when they come to call on me!" smiled Aunt Mary Moppit.

13 The Farmyard Chase

The farmer and his wife were having breakfast. "How quiet it is!" said the farmer as he munched his toast. "How peaceful!"

Then, without any warning, there came the sound of cackling and squawking, crowing and screeching from the farmyard outside.

The farmer's little boy needed some extra feathers for his Indian Chief's headdress, and was chasing the turkey round the yard.

Then all of a sudden the turkey turned round and began to chase the little boy - now it was his turn to yell and shout!

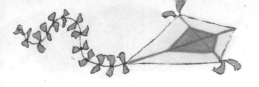 

Ashley's Dog

14

Ashley decided to train his little dog.

"First I shall teach him to bring me things," said Ashley.

"Always remember to be patient and kind," advised Ashley's mum.

Very soon the little dog learned to fetch a stick or a slipper, or even a newspaper.

One morning when Ashley opened the front door, his little dog had fetched not just one newspaper, but everybody's newspapers down the street.

Now Ashley has to spend all morning putting them back through the right doors!

Going Skating

15

Three little girls went to the ice rink. They had a marvellous time. Dolly skated to the music, Molly twirled round and round and Holly danced like a fairy.

All around them skaters were falling down and bumping into one another, which made Dolly, Molly and Holly squeal with laughter.

But when they left the ice rink to go home, Dolly tripped over the kerb, Molly walked into a lamppost and Holly fell up the front doorstep.

"We're safer on the ice rink," said the three girls as they rubbed their bruises.

The Wind Blows

One very windy day Ma and Pa Bramley put on warm clothes and went for a walk through their apple orchard.

The wind saw them coming and said to the sun. "I'm sure that I can blow Ma and Pa Bramley's coats right off!"

"Never!" smiled the sun and went behind a cloud.

So the wind began to blow. He howled through the branches of the apple trees, which made Ma and Pa Bramley button up their coats tightly.

"Let's go back inside!" gasped Pa who could hardly stand up.

"Right Pa!" puffed Ma as she turned up her coat collar.

So they both went back home, sat in front of the kitchen fire and ate roast apples filled with brown sugar and cream.

The Sun Shines

Next day Ma and Pa went for a walk in their apple orchard as usual.

At once the wind began to blow. "I'm sure I can make them take their coats off today!" he told the sun.

"Today it is my turn," smiled the sun as he came from behind a cloud. He shone so brightly that soon everywhere felt warm.

"Are you hot?" Ma Bramley asked Pa.

"Roasting!" replied Pa and began to take off his coat.

"Now the wind has gone, it feels like a summer day," said Ma and she took her coat off too.

"I win!" smiled the sun.

"So you do!" sighed the wind, and he blew away!

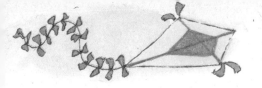

18 Sam's Finger Puppets

Sam was climbing over the fence and caught his best pair of gloves on a row of sharp nails.

"They're ruined!" cried Sam. "My gloves are good for nothing now."

"Don't throw them away!" said his sister. "If you cut them up we could make ten lovely finger puppets."

19 First Aid At The Zoo

A little monkey at the zoo fell out of a tree and grazed his arm.

Norah, the zoo keeper's wife, picked him up, rubbed some ointment on his arm and bandaged it up. Then she sat him on her knee, gave him a big hug and a kiss, just to make him feel better.

The zoo keeper bought him a lollipop and a book so Norah could read him a story.

Now all the other animals want a bandage although there is nothing wrong with them!

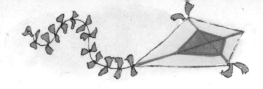

Along Came An Onion!

20

The carrot told a funny joke which made all the vegetables laugh.

The tomato laughed until he was red in the face, and so did the beetroot. The courgettes giggled and the radishes rolled about with laughter.

Then all of a sudden they started to cry. I wonder why?

Along came an onion, which brought tears to everyone's eyes!

21

Belinda Gets Wet

It was a wet and windy afternoon and Belinda the ragdoll was getting ready to go for a walk.

"Don't go out," said the other toys. "It's raining and you will get wet!"

But Belinda didn't listen, she went outside and soon got very wet indeed.

"My feet are soaking and my legs are all soggy!" she howled.

"You're a ragdoll Belinda," cried the other toys. "We told you not to go out in the rain!"

The little girl who owned Belinda found her soggy doll. She put her in the warm airing cupboard with the fluffy towels and soft pillows. And there Belinda stayed for several days.

The other toys felt sorry for her and came to see if she was alright, but Belinda was really enjoying herself tucked up in the warm, comfy airing cupboard.

22 Angelo And Lorenzo's Music

Angelo and Lorenzo lived next door to each other. Usually they were the best of friends, but all night long Angelo played the tuba which made Lorenzo very cross.

So, one day Lorenzo went out and bought a double bass.

What a din the two made. Angelo yelled at Lorenzo for making so much noise, and Lorenzo shouted at Angelo for playing out of tune.

Then one day they agreed to play together. They found that they could make such beautiful music, they never argued again!

23 Silly Billy

Billy the goat had two large horns. If he saw the farmer bending down, Billy would charge across the farmyard and butt him.

"That's not funny!" yelled the farmer angrily as he picked himself up. Then Billy would run off to see the farmer's wife because she spoiled him and gave him wine gums.

"You silly Billy," scolded the farmer's wife. "You can help me with my wool, and be useful for a change!"

Baby Bett Goes Shopping

24

Baby Bett Brown loved going on a trip to the supermarket.

"I think Baby Bett behaves very well when we are shopping!" said her dad.

"Then I shall do the shopping while you look after Baby Bett," said her mother with a smile.

Baby Bett still loves her trips to the supermarket. Do you think her dad does too?

I Wonder Who Lives There?

25

Helen the hamster was very inquisitive. She knew everybody that lived in the High Street, except for the very last house.

"I wonder who lives there?" Helen would say.

So one day she went down the path and knocked loudly on the door. Next she peeped through the windows and then she looked through the letter box...And what do you think she saw - two little bright eyes looking back at her! Then the door opened just a little way, and peering from behind was a pink nose and a pair of whiskers - just like Helen's. It was another hamster!

"I'm very shy!" whispered a tiny voice.

"And I'm very inquisitive!" laughed Helen, "so we should get on very well together!"...And they did.

26 The Gingerbread Girl

Bevis said that he would like to help his mother to bake.

"What would you like to make?" asked his mother. "Gingerbread men would be nice!"

Bevis shook his head. "No-one ever makes gingerbread girls," said Bevis, "so I shall make one of those for a change!"

When his mother took the gingerbread girl from the oven, she was thrilled. "She looks too good to eat. I shall thread her on a ribbon and hang her up in my kitchen. Well done Bevis!"

27 The Floating Dormouse

On windy days when the March wind blows and Dottie Dormouse is in a hurry, she puts on her hat and coat and goes outside to look for a patch of dandelions.

Then, very carefully she chooses the biggest dandelion clock, hangs onto the stem very tightly and floats off down the road.

And if she is very lucky, and the wind changes, she can float back home again!

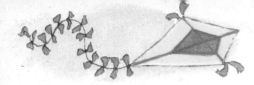

The Missing Pies

Gordon got up very early before the sun got hot. He baked lots of tasty pies and put them outside to cool, but later when he went to bring them inside, every single one had vanished!

Gordon looked everywhere.

"Have you seen my pies?" he asked Percy the pelican. But Percy didn't reply, his beak was too full!

Deep Sea Ride

28

29

"I'm tired of swimming around all day," said one little fish to the other. "I wish we had something to ride on!"

"You're absolutely right," agreed the other little fish. "Down at the bottom of the sea there are no cars or buses or trains, and definitely no bicycles!"

"Just a minute," chuckled the first little fish. "We do have sea horses!"

Ashley's Missing Seeds

30

Ashley planted lots of seeds in his garden, but nothing ever grew.

"I can't understand it!" said Ashley with a sigh.

But one day as he looked out of the window at his patch of brown earth, he understood why.

His little dog was digging up one side of the garden, his kitten was scratching the soil on the other side, and a flock of birds were pecking at the seeds in the middle.

"I think I shall have to plant my seeds in a window box," said Ashley, "they'll be safe there!"

Brandy's Cabin

31

In early spring, many of the bears on Big Bear Mountain were busy building log cabins to live in during the warm weather.

Brandy Bear, who was quite small, really wanted to help. So the big bears gave him a pile of small logs and his very own hammer and box of nails.

At the end of the day Brandy had made a tiny log cabin - just the right size for a mailbox!

Soon Brandy was making mailboxes for all the families on Big Bear Mountain.

1 Aunt Mary Moppit's Hat

"I do look forward to Eastertime," said Aunt Mary Moppit. "I shall make quite sure that I have a big chocolate rabbit and a big chocolate egg, but most of all I shall make sure that I have an enormous Easter hat!" And with that she trotted off to the hat shop to choose one.

Now when Aunt Mary Moppit returned home she was carrying the biggest hatbox you ever saw. Inside was an enormous Easter hat. It was far too big to go through the door, so she had to keep it in the porch outside.

"Listen to those birds singing!" Aunt Mary Moppit said humming as she made lunch. "It must be spring!"

It was when Aunt Mary Moppit went out to admire her Easter hat, that she found out why the birds were so cheerful. They were building a nest in her new hat!

"Not to worry!" she smiled, "I shall wear the hatbox instead!"

2 The Little Easter Bunny

Tom's baby sister was far too young for chocolate, so instead of an Easter egg, she was given a smart new outfit to keep the blustery spring winds away.

Do you think that when she wears her outfit people might think she's the Easter bunny? I think they might.

3 Mr. Magic's Easter Treat

When Mr. Magic did tricks for his family, he often pulled white rabbits out of his top hat and sometimes white doves that flew round and round his head.

But at Eastertide he takes his top hat, waves his magic wand, and pulls out chocolate rabbits and Easter eggs of every shape and size. His friends think this is magic!

4 The Easter Hare

On Easter morning some children go on an egg hunt to search for eggs hidden by the Easter hare.

Sometimes the eggs are made of chocolate, others are hard boiled with brightly coloured shells.

If you are lucky enough to go on an egg hunt, remember to look everywhere, for the Easter Hare is a crafty fellow and hides his eggs in the strangest places.

5 Sammy's Buggy Ride

Tricia was taking her dog Sammy for a walk when she noticed he was limping.

"We need to take Sammy to the vet," said her mother.

"He can ride in my old buggy!" suggested Tricia.

The vet bandaged Sammy's leg and in a few days he could walk properly - But he still likes to ride in Tricia's buggy!

The Little Lamb Finds His Mother

One spring morning the little brown cow saw a tiny lamb running into the farmyard.

"Are you my mother?" bleated the lamb when she saw the little brown cow.

"Moo!" replied the little brown cow. "I'm not your mother, but I'll help you to find her!"

Next the lamb ran up to a turkey who was strutting up and down the farmyard. "Are you my mother?" asked the lamb, but the turkey spread out his feathers and made such a loud gobbling noise that the lamb fell backwards into the the pigs trough.

"Are you my mother?" the lamb asked a fat pink pig.

"Oink! Oink!" snorted the pig and carried on eating.

"I'll never find my mother," bleated the lamb very loudly.

"Listen!" mooed the little brown cow. "I think I can hear her!" But the tiny lamb went on bleating.

All of a sudden his mother ran through the gate.

"Baa, baa, baa! There you are!" she called to her lamb. "I could hear you bleating and came to find you."

So the lamb said goodbye to the little brown cow and went home happily with his mother.

Ashley Learns To Write

On his first day at school Ashley learned to write 1, 2, 3. His mum and dad were very proud of Ashley, they thought he was so clever!

That night when they went into the bathroom they saw how well Ashley could write 1, 2, 3.

He had squeezed the numbers onto the bathroom mirror - in toothpaste!

Brandy's Nest Boxes

8

Brandy Bear had been very busy making mailboxes for all the folks who lived on Big Bear Mountain.

Now one day early in May, the bear who delivered the mail came to Brandy with a problem.

"I'm afraid I can't put letters into some of the boxes," said the mail bear scratching his head, "the birds are building nests inside!"

This gave Brandy an idea. He fetched his toolbox and straight away began to make the birds nest boxes of their very own!

Edward's Pyjamas

9

When Edward the flying elephant wanted to fly his plane, he could never tell which way the wind was blowing.

One day he saw his mother hanging out his pyjamas on the washing line and this gave Edward and idea.

He rummaged around in a drawer until he found an old pair of pyjamas that were too patched to wear.

Now Edward can tell exactly which way the wind is blowing and take off in safety.

The Wooden Spoon People

10

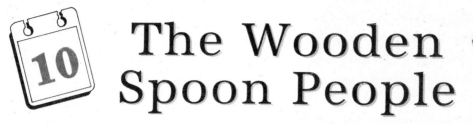

At night when everyone is fast asleep in bed and all the house is quiet, if you peep through the kitchen door you may be in for a surprise!

For this is the time the kitchen drawer slides open, and out come the Wooden Spoon people.

All night long they have fun and play, but the very second someone in the house wakes up, they jump back into the kitchen drawer and are ordinary wooden spoons again!

What Time Is It?

11

All the little sparrows that flew around the town square met at quarter to three.

"Is that the time you have your tea?" asked a pigeon looking down from the roof.

"Oh no!" twittered the little sparrows, very amused. "That's the only time we can sit in a row on the hands of the Town Hall clock!"

Belinda's Cats

12

Belinda's cats hated visitors. They kissed them and picked them up and squeezed them, they stroked their fur the wrong way and tickled them under the chin, they even poked and played with their whiskers. Belinda's cats hated it!

So when visitors arrived, Belinda's cats would pretend to be ornaments, until the visitors left for home!

The Green Doors

Angelo moved into the house next door to Lorenzo. The front doors of both houses were very shabby.

"I have half a tin of blue paint," said Angelo, "I hate blue!"

"I have half a tin of of yellow paint," said Lorenzo, "and I hate yellow!"

So the two of them mixed the paint together and painted their front doors, and at the same time became good friends.

What A Lot Of Chicks

One day in Spring the little speckled hen was sitting on her nest of twenty eggs. As she listened carefully she thought she heard a 'cheep', and another and another.

She jumped off her nest and would you believe it her twenty eggs had hatched into twenty fluffy chicks.

"Bless my soul!" squarked the little speckled hen. "However am I going to keep my eye on all of you?"

"Don't you worry!" said the farmer's wife. "I'll pop them in this drawer lined with straw for a day or two, then we can both keep our eye on them!"

15 Henry Waters The Flowers

It was Henry's job to look after the flowers in the garden. On hot days when the soil was dry, they needed lots of water.

When he used the hosepipe on the flower beds, Henry always checked that no-one was in the way - just in case they got a soaking!

But one day when he watered the window boxes, he forgot to look down. Someone knocking on the front door is getting very wet!

16 The Rooftop Home

Paul and Richard's bedroom was on the top floor of the house, right underneath the roof. The twins loved their attic bedroom. It was very quiet and private up there, far from the noise of the traffic below. But just lately Paul and Richard had heard very strange noises and they were both puzzled.

"It seems to be coming from the top of the roof," said Paul. So they opened the skylight a little way and took a look outside and what do you think they found?

Two pigeons had built a nest right on top of an old chimney pot. Paul and Richard could just see two eggs inside.

"The birds will be quite safe up here," whispered Paul, "and we'll be able to watch the baby birds when they hatch!"

17 The Missing Eggs

During the Easter holidays, Toby and Ted asked a few friends round for tea.

"Before they come," said their mother, "take this basket of chocolate eggs and hide them in the garden. Your friends will have fun finding them!"

Toby and Ted spent all morning hiding the eggs, and when their friends came they spent all afternoon looking for them. But no-one found a single egg!

Toby and Ted looked in all the places they had hidden the eggs, but they couldn't find them either!

Now when their mother went into the kitchen to make the tea, she found the chocolate eggs back in the basket. All except one - and there was Tibby just bringing it in through the cat-flap!

18 Clara's Chicks

Clara was helping to feed the chickens at Strawberry Farm when she got quite a surprise.

"Come quickly!" she shouted to the farmer's wife. "The chicks are swimming around in the hen's water bowl. Come quickly or they might drown!"

The farmer's wife rushed over, then began to laugh.

"They're ducklings Clara, not chicks. Ducklings can swim as soon as they are hatched. They're quite safe, so don't worry!"

The Twins' Present

The twins had a present. It came in a big flat box. They tore off the wrapping paper, and when they took of the lid they found some farm animals inside.

"They won't stand up!" said one of the twins.

"That's because they're flat!" said the other. "Whoever heard of flat farm animals?"

But when they took a closer look inside the box they understood why.

"It's a farm puzzle," cried the twins, "and all the flat animal shapes fit into the holes!"

Sidney Baby-sits

Sidney the penguin promised to baby-sit for one of the little seal pups .

"No problem!" said Sidney. "Leave him with me. We'll sit on the iceberg and I'll tell him some stories."

But the little seal pup had other ideas!

As soon as Sidney's back as turned, he jumped off the iceberg and swam far out to sea. Lucky for Sidney, a passing walrus brought him back.

"Baby-sitting isn't as easy as I thought," sighed Sidney, and he tied a string on to the little seal pup - just in case he wandered off again!

"I think I need a bit of help," said Sydney. So the rest of his friends on the iceberg stopped what they were doing and played with the little seal pup until his mother came back.

APRIL

21 Paddy The Park Keeper

Paddy the park keeper was a very happy fellow. He never frowned or looked sad, he laughed and smiled all day long.

"What makes you so happy?" everyone asked Paddy.

"I'll let you all into a little secret!" he replied. "Every morning before I unlock the park gates, I go on all the rides," giggled Paddy, "and that is why I love being a park keeper!"

22 The Mystery Behind The Fence

Eric and his sisters were playing in the park. Next to the park keeper's hut was a tall fence. "Look here!" yelled Eric to the girls. "There's a small hole in the fence. Let's take it in turns to look through, then we can see what's on the other side!"

When the children looked through the hole, they were so surprised they ran across the park to tell their mother what they had seen.

"I saw a cockerel that was bigger than me!" said one of the girls.

"I saw a real unicorn!" cried the other.

"And I saw a pink elephant!" gasped Eric. Their mother smiled. "We'll come back to the park tomorrow and solve the mystery!"

And when the children returned to the park the next day, this is what they found...A carousel with a pink elephant, a cockerel and a unicorn to ride on!

 23 The Cabin On Top Of The Mountain

A little old man and a little old woman lived in a cabin on top of the mountain.

"We are getting too old to live up here anymore," said the little old man, so they moved to the foot of the mountain.

"Our little cabin on top of the mountain will be so lonely," sighed the little old woman.

"I've already thought of that," said the little old man with a smile. "I shall tell all the people that climb the mountain there is food, warmth and shelter in our little cabin. Then it will never be empty or lonely."

The very first climbers that reached the little cabin on top of the mountain put a bright light on the roof, so the little old man and the little old woman could see it shining brightly as they sat in their new cabin at the foot of the mountain.

 24 Grandma's Favourite Teacup

One afternoon when Maisy's Grandma was busy chattering, she knocked her favourite china teacup off the table onto the floor.

"Poor Grandma!" cried Maisy. "You've had that teacup since you were a little girl."

"It's my own fault," said Grandma. "I should have taken more care!"

Very carefully Maisy picked up the pieces. She borrowed some of her dad's glue and she stuck the teacup together.

"You've made a good job of that," Dad said, "but don't put hot tea in it, will you?"

But Maisy had a better idea. She bought a little flowering plant that just fitted into the china teacup.

Now Maisy's Grandma can look at her favourite cup every day, although she drinks her tea from a brand new one!

25 Too Many Cooks

Three busy cooks had so much work to do, they decided to help each other.

"I'll make a big pot of soup!" said one.

"I'll make a great bowl of spaghetti!" said another.

"And I'll make a huge bowl of custard!" said the third.

All went well until they began to argue.

"Your soup tastes awful!" said one, and added some sugar.

"Your spaghetti smells dreadful!" said another, and added some pepper.

"And your custard is lumpy!" said the third, and added some salt.

It wasn't very long before the customers complained and wouldn't pay their bills. So the three busy cooks had to make sandwiches for everyone, and agreed never to argue again!

26 Fizzy Grizzly Goes Shopping

Fizzy Grizzly went to the store to buy lots of cans of his favourite fizzy drink. He took a trolley and walked through the store taking great care not to bump into the shoppers.

He felt in his pocket to make sure he had enough money, and was about to fill his trolley.

"Take the cans from the top of the pile Fizzy!" yelled the store manager. "Please don't take them from the bottom!"

Too late! Fizzy has filled his trolley a lot faster than he thought!

27 Hurrah For Buzz Beaver

It had rained for days and days, and the stream that ran through the forest was as wide as a river.

"We must build a dam at once!" said the Chief Beaver, "or the lower part of the forest will be flooded and the animals will have no homes!"

Now to cut down trees, beavers have to use their strong front teeth.

"This will take far too long!" cried the Chief Beaver as he watched the water rising.

Then through the trees came Buzz Beaver with his chain saw. He cut down the trees they needed in next to no time. The dam was built and the forest was saved.

28 Sylvia Snail

One sunny morning as Sylvia Snail was crawling slowly across the lawn, she met a shiny green beetle.

"Where do you live?" asked the beetle politely.

"Can't you guess?" said Sylvia with a smile.

Further on she met a dragonfly.

"Do you live near here?" the dragonfly asked as he hovered over the snail.

"You don't know either!" said Sylvia with surprise.

Along came a velvety bumble bee. "Do tell us where you live!" he buzzed.

Sylvia was amazed. "I'll give you a clue," she said. "I'm just like the turtle and the tortoise!"

But the others just shook their heads.

"I carry my house on my back," laughed Sylvia. "My shell is my home!"

29 The Mischievous Little Bear Cub

Young Brandy the bear went to visit his Aunt Babs who lived on the other side of Big Bear mountain. He took his tool box along, just in case she needed something mending.

"Oh dear!" said Brandy as he opened his aunt's front door. "She sounds rather cross this morning."

No wonder - her baby bear cub was up to all sorts of mischief.

"My goodness!" Brandy gasped as he gazed around the room. "How can one little bear have done all this damage?"

"Quite easily!" replied Aunt Babs with a sigh. "He's always into mischief!"

So there and then Brandy opened his tool box, collected some pieces of wood and set to work.

By lunchtime he had finished. "Now you can get on with your work," Brandy told Aunt Babs. "Your little cub will be quite safe and out of mischief!"

30 New Beds For The Rabbits

Mrs. Grey Rabbit had a problem. She had a very large family and her burrow was quite small. What made things worse, all her children wanted to sleep in bunk beds!

"If you all have bunk beds," sighed Mrs. Grey Rabbit, "there will be no room for you to play with your toys on the floor!"

What a problem!

Then Mr. Grey Rabbit made all the little rabbits sleep on the lounge floor in sleeping bags for a whole week, while he altered the bedroom.

Now everyone is happy. There is plenty of space to play with toys on the floor and every little rabbit has a comfy new bed!

1 The First Day Of May

On the first day of May, countryfolk like to welcome the spring by dancing round the maypole.

Some of the young animals had been practising for weeks until they were perfect.

At first the maypole dance went very well. Everyone danced in and out of the pretty ribbons that hung from the top of the maypole.

Then some of the frogs from the pond nearby decided to join in.

Oh dear! I think things seem to be getting in a bit of a muddle!

2 Grandma's Speckled Hen

"When I was a little girl," said Dean's grandma, "I lived on a farm and we kept lots of speckled hens that laid beautiful brown eggs!"

"Do you miss your hens Grandma?" asked Dean.

"I certainly do!" said Grandma with a sigh. "I'm far too old to keep hens now, especially in my tiny flat!"

Dean felt quite sorry for his grandma. So the next time he went shopping, he saw just the thing to remind Grandma of the speckled hens she kept in days gone by.

3 Nigel Gets Into Mischief

Nigel was always getting into mischief. One day he fell out of the apple tree and hurt his arm. He had to go to hospital and have it X-rayed, then a nurse put Nigel's arm in a sling.

"Hopefully that will keep you out of mischief for a while," said Nigel's mother.

But she was wrong. Nigel had just remembered something in his back pocket. "My new sling will make a perfect home for my pet frog," said Nigel with a grin.

4 The Bunnies' Bedtime

Mrs. Grey Rabbit had a big family. The three youngest bunnies were so small they still slept in cradles.

"I need three hands to rock them to sleep!" sighed Mrs. Grey Rabbit, and the three youngest bunnies began to cry all at once.

Then Mr. Grey Rabbit got out his tool box and a length of wood. In next to no time he had solved the problem.

Now all is peace and quiet in the Grey Rabbits' burrow!

Rolo's Missing Nose

Rolo the clown was getting ready for his circus act. First he pulled on his baggy trousers and his giant size boots. Next he put on his clown's jacket and his silly shiny hat, and last of all he put on his make-up and bright red nose.

But oh dear, where was his nose? Quickly Rolo searched the box where his spare red noses were kept...It was empty!

Rolo searched everywhere. Every red nose had disappeared.

"For the very first time," said Rolo with a sad look on his face, "I shall have to go into the circus ring without my red nose!"

As he sat behind the curtains waiting for his act to begin, Rolo could hear the applause for all the other circus performers, but somehow it seemed different.

The audience screamed with laughter at the trapeze artists, and when the lion performed, everyone had hysterics.

"How very strange," said Rolo puzzled. "Everyone usually gasps at the trapeze artists and the lions, no-one ever laughs!"

But when Rolo peeped behind the curtains he understood why. Everyone in the circus was wearing one of Rolo's red noses!

Rolo's Photo

6

Rolo thought it would be a great idea to take a photograph of the circus folk for his album.

"You're going to throw water all over us!" shouted the lion tamer, and he pointed to a big bucket next to Rolo's camera.

"The bucket's empty, I promise!" joked Rolo and he turned it upside down.

So everyone got into position and Rolo looked through the camera. As he pressed the button, water squirted everywhere soaking everyone!

"The bucket was empty, but this is my trick camera!" laughed Rolo the clown.

Tiny Tiger Tim

7

Tiny Tiger Tim loved to go into the circus ring. He wanted to learn tricks or juggle, or maybe walk the tightrope.

The circus people tried to teach him, but Tiny Tiger Tim was hopeless.

"I wish I could make the audience clap and cheer for me," sighed poor Tim.

"I know a way you can do that," laughed the ringmaster.

So that night, halfway through the circus, Tiny Tiger Tim came round with giant ice creams for everyone, and that got the biggest cheer of all!

The Leaking Watering Can

Howard went into the garden to water the flowers and found that his watering can was leaking. "Don't throw it away!" said Howard to his dad. "I'm really fond of my watering can, it's such a shame it has a hole in it."

So Howard kept his watering can and turned it into a plant holder as you can see. Some people put plants in the strangest containers!

Edgar's Whistle

Edgar found a whistle, it made a marvellous sound.

He blew it when he passed the school playground and all the children ran across to see what was the matter.

He blew it near the kennels, and all the dogs jumped up and started barking.

Then he blew it as he passed the sports field which made the footballers bump into one another.

"It must be a magic whistle!" remarked Edgar blowing it loudly near his dad's ear.

"If it's magic, then watch it disappear!" said Dad crossly, and he locked poor Edgar's whistle in the top drawer!

10 Susie's New Pencil

Susie had a new pencil. With it she drew a picture of her mum and dad, then she drew her cat, her dog and her black and white rabbit.

She gave her pictures to her little brother and they made him laugh!

Susie left her new pencil on the floor and her little brother drew a wiggly line all over the kitchen wall which made Susie laugh!

But it didn't make Mum and Dad laugh at all!

11 Abigail's Cat

Abigail's cat was often naughty. She jumped up on the kitchen units and licked the butter. (If someone had forgotten to put the lid on the butter dish).

If she got the chance, Abigail's cat would drink from the milk jug. What a dreadful habit!

Now Abigail has made a special cover for the milk jug. So her cat will have to drink milk from her saucer like all good cats should!

12 The Voles Take Off

The vole triplets had been to visit their grandma deep in the middle of the wood.

It had been bright and sunny when they set out but dark clouds had gathered and soon there was a terrible storm.

When it was time to return home, the three little voles stood on the bank of the stream in despair.

"We walked across the stepping stones this morning, but now they've vanished!" they cried.

"I'll fetch Mr. Grey Badger," hooted the owl. "He'll know what to do!"

It wasn't long before the badger arrived on the scene with the answer to the voles' problem.

He blew up a big balloon and fixed a tiny basket underneath. Then in jumped the three little voles. They gently floated over the stream and arrived back safely home to their mother.

13 Busy Betsy

Betsy was busy all day long. She got up at the crack of dawn. She washed mountains of clothes all morning and ironed them in the afternoon. Then she spent all the evening packing them neatly into cases and bags.

"Have you got all your doll's clothes ready yet Betsy?" smiled her mum. "We are going on holiday first thing in the morning!"

14 Messenger Mole Takes A Nap

Messenger Mole was scurrying through the wood one day with a very important letter. All of a sudden he remembered it was lunch-time. So he sat down on a little mound, put his very important letter on the grass and ate some of his lunch.

It had been a very busy morning, so Messenger Mole thought he would take a little nap.

When he woke up, Messenger Mole was just in time to see his very important letter and the rest of his lunch slowly moving across the grass.

I don't think Messenger Mole will go to sleep on an ant hill again, do you?

15 It's Raining, It's Pouring!

It poured with rain all day and everyone tried very hard not to get wet.

Mushrooms can come in very handy, you can shelter underneath and keep perfectly dry. But what happens when you have to go home for tea?

It's time to pick a flower or catch a passing leaf!

The Penguins Build A Castle

16

"You can't make sandcastles on an iceberg," said Sidney the penguin to his sisters one day.

"We could build an igloo," said Chrissy.

"We could make a snowman," said Sissy.

But Sidney shook his head!

"How about an ice-cream castle?" suggested Missy. "Then everyone can help us eat it when it's finished!"

Baby Bear Goes Hiking

17

Babs Bear often went hiking on Big Bear Mountain. She liked to walk through the forest and explore the tracks that led up the mountain, but there was just one snag - her baby bear cub!

He was full of mischief and would run off and hide, and sometimes get lost. But one day Babs found just the right thing to keep her baby bear cub out of trouble!

18 The Grasshopper Learns To Count

A bright green grasshopper sat chirping in the long grass. "I shall never learn to count," he moaned. "I can't even count up to ten, I'm such a dunce!"

"Don't worry!" chorused the ten bright ladybirds. "Watch us and you'll soon learn."

First they found a daisy with ten petals, then they flew around and landed one by one. They did this lots of times and the bright green grasshopper counted out loud, one, two, three, four, five, six, seven, eight, nine, ten.

"I never realised I was so good at counting," he chirped. "Thanks ladybirds, all ten of you!"

19 Willy The Worm

"Why do you live underground?" the blue butterfly asked Willy the worm when he poked his head through the soil one day.

So that day, Willy decided to take a look at the world above ground. He heard bees buzzing, mosquitoes droning, caterpillars munching, centipedes stamping all their feet and butterflies flapping their wings loudly.

"It's far too noisy up here!" cried Willy and wriggled back underground.

20 Norah's Bit Of Peace And Quiet

Sometimes Norah the zoo keeper's wife liked a bit of peace and quiet.

"I would like somewhere out of the way, where I could sit and knit for a while!" said Norah.

So the zoo keeper built her a tree house of her very own she could reach by a rope ladder.

"Now you can knit in peace," smiled the zoo keeper. "No-one will bother you!"

Somehow I think Norah will have plenty of company don't you?

21 A Fruity Tale!

"It's far too hot today!" said the strawberry.

"I'm almost boiling!" gasped the apple.

"Look at me, I'm sweating!" puffed the pear.

"I'm luckier than all of you," bragged the banana. "I can take my coat off!"

Clumsy Claude

22

Claude was very clumsy, he tripped over everything in his house.

He banged his head on the kitchen cupboard, he stubbed his toe on the bed, he hurt his knees falling upstairs and he trapped his fingers in the drawers. Clumsy Claude!

"I need a house like a big soft cushion," cried poor Claude. "I shall have one made right away, then I can be as clumsy as I like!"

Mike's Spare Tyre

"I shall have to buy a new spare tyre," said Mike's dad as he looked inside the car boot.

"This spare tyre is useless. I must get a new one just in case I have a puncture!"

"I don't think it's useless," said Mike, "can I have it?"

So Mike took the spare tyre away, and next time his dad went into the garden he saw his old spare tyre.

Now it's very useful indeed!

24 Hot Dogs

Two little hot dogs took part in a race. They ran so fast that no-one could catch them.

They ran all morning and they ran all afternoon.

At last they reached the finishing line and came first in the race.

"Now we really are hot dogs!" they laughed mopping their brows.

25 Keep Quiet Please!

It was late spring and every time the woodland folk used the stepping stones to cross the stream, Otto the Otter would poke his head above the water.

"Ssshh!" whispered Otto. "Quiet please!"

After a little while the woodland folk could see why Otto was being so fussy. He was keeping a family of young kingfishers safe, until they were old enough to fly!

Blossom Time

All the baby animals that had been born on the farm in springtime had never seen snow.

"What does it look like?" asked the lamb.

"When can we see some?" said the foal.

All of a sudden the farmer's wife thought of an idea. She took the young animals along to Ma and Pa Bramley's apple orchard.

The trees were covered in blossom and hundreds of petals were gently falling to the ground, just like snow.

Ma and Pa Bramley laughed as they sat with the animals under the trees. "Snow may look like blossom, but it's cold and wet and freezing!"

"We can hardly wait for winter to come!" laughed the animals and then ran off to play in the warm sunshine.

27 Fly Little Bird!

It was late spring and lots of baby birds were learning to fly for the first time.

All over the wood little birds were sitting on branches plucking up the courage to jump off and fly away.

Here's one little bird making absolutely sure that he will have a safe landing!

28 Rosalind's Books

Rosalind loved books. She could only read a few words, so she liked books with lots of pictures best.

Now Rosalind was very small and all her books were large, so it was very difficult for her to read them.

One day, in a bookshop she saw the same stories and pictures in tiny books.

"These are just the right size for me," cried Rosalind, "until I grow a bit bigger!"

29 Mitzi's Shadow

Mitzi was trying hard to jump over the rainbow, so was her shadow.

Then a big black cloud came floating by and blotted out the sun. Mitzi's shadow disappeared and so did the rainbow.

30 Bevis And His Badges

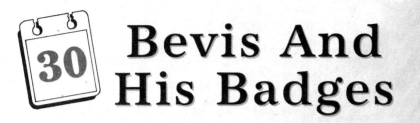

Bevis went shopping to buy a new sweater.

"Would you like stripes or zig-zags, or one with a pattern all over?" asked his mother.

"I would like a perfectly plain one with no fancy bits on at all!" said Bevis most definitely.

"If your mind's made up, a plain sweater it shall be," said his mother.

When she saw Bevis in his sweater for the first time, she got quite a surprise.

"I needed a plain sweater to show off all my badges!" smiled Bevis.

31 Baby Bett's Tulips

Dad took Baby Bett Brown into the garden to look at his prize tulips. He put her in the middle of the lawn, just to keep her out of mischief for a moment, while he went indoors to fetch his camera.

"I shall take a picture of Baby Bett and my tulips!" said Dad proudly.

I don't think this is quite the picture Dad wanted, do you?

JUNE

1 Clarissa's Flowers

The farmer and his wife warned Clarissa the duck never to go outside the farmyard, but Clarissa was such a scatterbrain, she soon forgot.

Mr. Fox on the other hand, was always on the look out for Clarissa, for he loved roast duck for his dinner.

"I shall go to the meadow and pick the farmer's wife a bunch of flowers," quacked Clarissa one bright summer morning. So she took some scissors and a long length of ribbon and set off.

Now Mr. Fox had overheard Clarissa's plan, so he rushed over to the meadow and waited for her.

Clarissa took so long to reach the meadow that Mr. Fox fell fast asleep in the warm sunshine.

The meadow was full of bright summer flowers and soon Clarissa had picked a beautiful bunch for the farmer's wife.

"I'll just tie them up with the ribbon," quacked Clarissa.

But she couldn't find it anywhere. "I must have dropped it in the meadow," said the scatterbrained duck. "I'll hurry home and find some more!"

Little did Clarissa know that two bluebirds had spied Mr. Fox fast asleep in the meadow. They flew down and tied him up tightly with the ribbon, so Clarissa got back to the farmyard safe and sound!

Spot Goes On A Picnic

Everyone loves a picnic, especially on a warm afternoon down by the river.

"I think I'll go for a swim before I eat," said Spot the dog as he jumped in the water. "I might even fetch a stick if someone throws one in!"

So Spot paddled around in the river until he saw all the delicious food being set out on the grass.

"Come on out Spot!" cried his owner from the bank, "Teas's ready!"

So Spot hurried out of the water and shook himself hard.

Oh dear Spot, now everyone has had a shower as well as a picnic!

The Wet Sports Day

On school sports day it poured with rain.

"We can't have the sack race," said the teacher, "its far too wet!"

"Never mind!" shouted the children. "We can still have the three-legged race because that's our favourite."

"Now how are you going to do that?" asked their teacher.

"Easy!" cried the children "We'll run the race under our umbrellas!"

4 Dottie Visits The Town

When Dottie Dormouse went to town to stay with her cousin Dorah, she was quite worried. "I've never stayed in a town before," said Dottie, "I'll get lost in the streets and I'll never ever find your house!"

"Don't worry Dottie," laughed Dorah. "I live at number three in the middle of lots of other houses that all look alike."

This made poor Dottie look even more worried.

"Remember number three," smiled Dorah, "and you're bound to find me!"

5 The Gigantic Model

Toby and Ted made a gigantic model at school. It was made out of cardboard boxes, pipes, tubes and all sorts of useful rubbish.

At the end of term when the classroom was cleared for the holidays, Toby and Ted were asked to take their model home.

"It's far too big to fit into the car!" said Toby and Ted's mother as she stared at the gigantic model. "Perhaps you ought to leave it at school!"

"Never!" cried Toby and Ted, who were very proud of their model. "We'll get it home somehow!"

And this is how they did it!

6 Bert's Roadroller

Bert and his roadroller lived at the bottom of a very steep hill. When the weather was warm and sunny, the road in front of Bert's house was busy all day long.

Then Bert would sit outside his house watching the traffic and waiting for cars towing caravans. For Bert knew that when they reached the bottom of the very steep hill, they would need him and his roadroller to give them a push right to the top!

7 Bert Helps The Circus

When the circus was in town, Bert and his roadroller were always busy.

First a road had to be laid for all the circus vehicles to drive on. Then the field had to be flattened where the Big Top was going to stand.

But the most important of all, Bert and his roadroller had to press the extra long trousers of the stilt walker because no-one had an ironing board that long!

8 The Little Brown Cow Gets Lost

Once upon a time there was a little brown cow. In early summer when the meadows were full of rich green grass and scented clover, the little brown cow would often wander far away from the farm.

She was so busy smelling the flowers and eating the grass, she forgot the time and sometimes found herself far from home when darkness fell.

It took the farmer ages to find her in the dark and there was a long walk back.

One day the farmer's wife thought of a good idea. She bought a big bell and fastened it around the little brown cow's neck on a fancy ribbon - now everyone can hear where she is!

9 Pretty Pansies

Aunt Min had a window box full of pretty pansies.

The lady next door said that hers were much prettier.

So the very next time she came round, Aunt Min's pansies stuck out their tongues and she never came back again!

10 The Clown's Plain Suit

Zolo the clown washed his circus suit and hung it out to dry. But the sun went behind a cloud and Zolo's suit was still wet when it was time to get ready for the circus.

"I shall have to go in an ordinary plain suit," gasped Zolo. "A clown in a plain suit - it's unheard of!"

All of a sudden the sun came out and all the beautiful butterflies in Zolo's garden settled all over the clown.

"Now I look perfect for the circus," laughed Zolo and off he went!

11 Helen's Special Basket

Helen the hamster was very inquisitive. One day as she was walking in the meadow she spied a very interesting looking basket.

"Now wonderful!" squeaked Helen as she hopped inside. "It has little plates, cups and saucers, tiny knives and forks, and silver spoons."

Then Helen's nose wrinkled as she sniffed around in the bottom of the basket. "How lovely!" she gasped as she reached out her paw, "here are sandwiches and pies and cakes and biscuits!"

So inquisitive Helen tried them all. She ate so much and felt so full she fell fast asleep!

The next thing she knew, the lid on the basket had been closed up tight, and she was being lifted up into the air.

"Let me out!" squealed Helen as loudly as she could, but no-one seemed to hear.

Quickly Helen picked up a fork and pushed it hard against the lid. Suddenly the picnic basket flew open and Helen was tipped out onto the grass.

"I'll never be inquisitive again!" said Helen, very thankful to be free. "But the food in the basket was delicious!"

And she scampered back for tea.

Pippin's Mud Bath

Pippin the pig thought she was very beautiful. This little pig lived with Ma and Pa Bramley, and they thought she was beautiful too!

One day Pippin read something in her beauty magazine that made her snort with delight.

'Take a bath in mud, and it will leave your skin soft and glowing!' it said.

So straight away Pippin found a big patch of mud and rolled around until she was completely covered.

"Don't come any closer!" gasped Ma Bramley in horror when she saw how filthy her little pig was.

"I'm supposed to look beautiful," squealed Pippin very upset.

"You just look grubby to me," laughed Pa Bramley, which made Pippin squeal even louder and big tears roll down her muddy cheeks.

So Ma and Pa Bramley fetched some apple-scented bubble bath, filled all their watering cans with warm water, and Pippin was pink and clean in no time.

"You're beautiful enough as you are," said Ma Bramley giving Pippin a big hug.

And from that day to this Pippin has never had a mud bath again!

13 In A Jam

Gordon was very strong. He could bend iron bars and lift heavy weights high above his head.

One day he got caught in a traffic jam. He couldn't move forward and he couldn't move backwards.

"I can't stay here all day," Gordon said, "I'm in a hurry!"

So he picked up his car and walked away!

14 Ludo The Lazy Lizard

"I don't like walking, I don't like strolling, I can't stand jogging and I absolutely hate running!" Ludo the lazy lizard told everyone he met...

"But this is a perfect way to get around for a lazy lizard like me!"

15

Ophelia The Octopus

Ophelia joined the orchestra and the conductor asked her what she could play.

First Ophelia played the xylophone, then she played a tune on the piano, next she picked up eight drumsticks and played four drums at a time.

"We need someone to play the harp," said the conductor. "I'm sure you'll do it very well Ophelia!"

16

The Untidy Little Rabbits

Every single one of the little grey rabbits was very untidy. Mrs. Grey Rabbit was always complaining.

So one day she went out and bought a special coat stand.

"Now you will be able to hang up all your things and keep the place tidy," she said with a smile.

The little grey rabbits tried very hard to do as their mother had asked, but somehow I don't think they will be able to manage it, do you?

Let's Pretend

17

Dolly, Molly and Holly liked playing 'Let's Pretend'.

This morning they were pretending to be housewives. Dolly pretended to sweep the floor, Molly pretended to dust and Holly pretended to clean the windows.

Their mother thought it was great fun and asked if she could play. Then she filled the kitchen sink with water.

"I'll pretend I've hurt my hand and can't do any work, so Dolly can wash the pots, Molly can dry them and Holly can pack them away!" she laughed.

Laura's Bicycle

18

"I wish I had a bicycle," said Laura to her mum.

Her mum heaved a big sigh. "It must be the hundredth time you've said that this morning."

"But I really would like a bicycle," said Laura once more.

"If you mention the word 'bicycle' again Laura," said mum very fed up, "I think I shall scream!"

But when Mum saw what Laura had done, she didn't scream, she laughed, and in a little while Laura got her bicycle!

19 Miss Mole To The Rescue

Messenger Mole had to deliver a special parcel deep in the heart of the forest. He had never been down such dark overgrown paths before. He tripped over the tangled tree roots, and his shiny gold uniform got caught up in the thorny brambles.

Poor Messenger Mole felt very frightened and alone. Then he remembered the tiny mobile phone fixed to his belt. Quickly he pressed the emergency button.

In next to no time he heard a scrabbling and a scratching. He looked down at his feet and out popped his aunt, Miss Mole, from beneath the ground.

"You silly mole!" she said when she saw her nephew looking so frightened. "No-one lives this deep in the forest. You must have got the wrong address. Come back home with me and we'll find out who this parcel is really for!"

So Messenger Mole followed his aunt back through the mole's underground passages, and never ventured so deep into the forest again!

20 Tenpin Bowling

Alvin and Addy Armadillo looked forward to Saturday night, because that was the night they went tenpin bowling.

Every time they played, they won. Do you know why?

They simply rolled themselves up into a ball and knocked all the pins down in one go!

Naughty Edgar

21

Edgar was a naughty boy, especially at school.

So first thing every morning, Edgar's teacher would ask him to empty his pockets.

It's quite surprising what she found...a toy car, a pocket game, a water pistol, a pea shooter, trick spiders and beetles by the box-full. She even asked Edgar to take off his watch, which played loud tunes all through her lessons.

"Right Edgar!" said the teacher. "Your pockets are empty, expect for a clean handkerchief, you can't get into mischief with that!"

But she was wrong! Edgar folded it into a cloth mouse to tease the girls with. You naughty boy Edgar!

The Jiggling Jelly

22

Minnie and Winnie's Uncle Fred lived in a house by the railway line. Many years ago Uncle Fred was a train driver and he still loved to see and hear the trains. When they thundered past, Uncle Fred's whole house shook. Minnie and Winnie thought it was very exciting.

Best of all, when Uncle Fred set the tea and the express went past, the jelly jiggled so much it almost jumped off the table!

23

At The Market

The alligator and the crocodile went to the market.

"I must have lots of vegetables!" said the alligator firmly.

"And I must have lots of fruit!" said the crocodile quite determined.

"Vegetables!" yelled the alligator.

"Fruit!" the crocodile snapped back, and the two began to quarrel.

"Catch!" cried the man behind the stall.

Now the alligator has lots of vegetables and the crocodile has lots of fruit!

24

Bruno's Bark

Bruno was a guard dog. He was big and strong and looked very fierce, but burglars were not afraid of him at all. Can you guess why?

When Bruno barked he gave a tiny woof which didn't frighten burglars one little bit!

Now one day when Bruno was on guard, he gave a tiny little woof as he passed a huge hollow tube. The tiny little woof echoed through the tube until it sounded like a great big fierce bark.

Now all the burglars run away from Bruno the minute they hear him.

25 The Busy Farmer

"I'm very busy today," said the farmer. "Everyone must lend a hand. I have a trailer full of hay that needs unloading!"

He drove his tractor into the middle of the farmyard. "Where is everybody?" asked the farmer gazing round.

"There's never anyone here when there's work to be done!"

26 The Great White Sea Hen

Two bird-watchers were looking for the Great White Sea Hen, so they waited and watched every day for a whole week.

"There's no such bird!" said one of the bird-watchers and they went away very disappointed.

Then the Great White Sea Hen flapped her wings and flew back home, giggling all the way!

Six Little Caterpillars

27

Six little caterpillars sat on a leaf. They asked the insects passing by, "What do you do all day?"

"We flutter and fly!" said the butterflies.

"We buzz!" said the flies.

"We hum!" said the bees.

Then the insects asked the six little caterpillars, "What do you do all day?"

"We munch and crunch, we nibble and chew, we eat everything in sight, yum yum!" they answered.

Then the six little caterpillars gobbled up their leaf and moved on to the next one!

Rhino Pays A Visit

28

Gordon went downstairs one morning and unlocked his front door.

"It must be jammed!" said Gordon, and he pushed against the door with all his might. But however hard he tried, the door wouldn't open.

"I'll have to fetch a screwdriver," said Gordon standing back.

"Anybody at home?" called Rhino. "I've been trying to open this door for ages.

29 Ashley's Egg

Ashley was ready for school. He looked very smart.

As he was eating his egg for breakfast, his school tie dangled in the soft, runny egg yolk.

Oh dear Ashley! I don't think that is the right way to get rid of the stain. Whatever will your mum say?

30 The Mascots

Two little chipmunks loved baseball. They had hours of fun playing with a tiny bat and ball, but most of all, they loved going to a baseball game.

The seats in the stadium were far too big for the little chipmunks, so they climbed up on top of the fence and had a wonderful view.

The baseball team often saw the two little chipmunks watching the game, and one day the captain came across to ask them a favour.

"Will you be our mascots and come to all the games?" said the captain.

The two little chipmunks fell over with excitement.

Now the team wins all the time with the two little chipmunks as mascots!

Good Morning Mr. Wolf

1

One bright morning two fat little pigs decided to go to town. Now on the way there, the road went straight past Mr. Wolf's front door.

"I know!" giggled one little pig. "We can fool old Mr. Wolf if we wear masks and go to town in disguise!"

So that is what they did. As they passed Mr. Wolf's house they smiled and waved and wished him good morning!

"We've tricked him!" they sniggered as they trotted down the road.

But had they? The two little pigs had covered their faces but they had forgotten their backs.

Run fast little pigs, I think Mr. Wolf may recognise those two little curly tails!

A.B.C.

2

"What does that word say?" Amy asked her mother.

"You must learn your alphabet, then you will know which letters make different words."

"Letters are boring!" said Amy. "I'll never remember them."

Now the letters in Amy's book overheard what she said, so that night when the little girl fell asleep, they came out of the book to play.

Next morning when Amy woke up, she remembered some of the letters and could spell short words in her book.

"Mummy," she said as she went downstairs. "Last night I had the funniest dream - all about letters!"

3 I Spy A Tiger

"Are we nearly there?" asked Woody. He always asked this question two streets from his house. Woody got very bored on long trips in the car with his older sisters and Mum and Dad.

"Why don't you play 'I Spy'?" asked Mother but his sisters always cheated!

One day as they drove through the countryside playing 'I Spy' the girls were busy spying everything. "I spy a red car, I spy a church tower, I spy a windmill."

Suddenly Woody cried out, "I spy a tiger and it's smiling at me!"

"Liar, Liar, pants on fire!" screamed Woody's sisters and by the time their mother had calmed them down, the tiger was left far behind.

Half an hour later when Dad pulled into a car park, he switched on the car radio.

"A tiger has escaped from Longbridge Zoo and may be heading for the main road!"

Woody sat with a wide grin on his face. "I told you I spied a tiger, so there!"

4 You Can Fly

Lots of little ladybirds were playing on a leaf. Suddenly a strong gust of wind blew the leaf high into the air.

"Help!" shrieked the little ladybirds as they clung to the leaf. "Help! Help! Help!"

Then they heard their mother's voice. "Don't forget little ladybirds you can fly!"

Iggy Frog

5

Once upon a time there lived a very shy little green frog.

"I wish you would hop off and find some friends to play with," suggested Iggy's mum.

"I have a friend," shrilled Iggy, "he lives under this lily pad!"

So his mum left him alone, because she had lots to do.

All day long Iggy gazed at his friend. He smiled and waved, and his friend smiled and waved back.

Suddenly one day a silver minnow stuck his head out of the water.

"Oh no!" cried Iggy "you've frightened my friend away!"

"Silly Iggy," laughed the silver minnow, "that wasn't a friend, it was your reflection. Now hop off that lily pad, come with me and find some new friends!"

A Fishy Story

6

Iggy Frog and his friend the silver minnow were swimming along under the water one day.

"What are those lines trailing above us?" Iggy asked Minnow.

"Don't go near them!" begged the little minnow swimming quickly away, "they are fishermen's lines to catch fish like me!"

Iggy thought for a while. We'll give those fishermen something to catch instead of minnows.

7 Summer Showers

One summer's day the weather was very hot, even the zoo keeper had to take off his jacket and wear a shady hat.

When lunchtime came the animals were too hot to eat.

"No-one can keep cool today," said the zoo keeper's wife. "Even the water in the penguins' pool is warm enough to wash in!"

"We would all like a refreshing shower," chorused the animals, "we're so hot and sticky!"

At that very moment it began to rain. Big drops of cold water poured down on to the animals, and very soon they felt much better.

"Just a minute!" shouted the zoo keeper, "It's not raining at all."

"Just doing our bit to help!"...It was the elephants squirting water from their long trunks.

8 Willy Woodpecker's Headache

Willie Woodpecker was learning to tap holes in trees, he was just a beginner.

"If you tap very hard and very fast," said his father, "you will soon bore a big hole in any tree, just like me!"

"Right!" nodded Willie and flew away towards the woods,

In a little while he was back. "I don't think I shall make a very good woodpecker," sighed Willie, "it gives me a headache!"

"Woodpeckers don't get headaches," said his father looking rather worried. "Let's see just what you have been up to," and he flew after Willie towards the wood.

"No wonder you have a headache," laughed Willie's father. "You've been tapping on a metal flagpole instead of a tree you silly Willie!"

9 Baby Hedgehog Keeps Out Of Mischief

Mrs. Hedgehog had a big family, ten small hedgehogs, what a lot to look after!

Of all her ten children, Baby Hedgehog was the most trouble, especially on washing day.

"I'm only trying to help," said Baby Hedgehog as he got under his mother's feet for the hundredth time.

At last Mrs. Hedgehog came up with a bright idea. She hung a pair of clean dry socks on her washing line, and Baby Hedgehog is kept out of mischief, at least for half an hour!

10 The End Of Term Cake

In the summer when school is at an end, everybody looks forward to their long summer holiday.

The little hedgehogs could hardly wait. Today was their very last day of term. Baby Hedgehog was too young to go to school and could hardly wait for his brothers and sisters to come home.

"I won't be on my own after today," he smiled. "I'll have plenty of friends to play with."

"Shall we make a cake to celebrate?" asked Mrs. Hedgehog. "If we hurry, it will be ready by the time they leave school."

So they set to work, and when the cake came out of the oven, it was perfect!

"I'll do the decoration!" said Baby Hedgehog as he climbed up high on a stool to reach the kitchen table.

He used up all the icing sugar and a whole box of chocolate drops...And when the other little hedgehogs came home, this is the wonderful cake they found on the table to celebrate the end of term.

11 Jessie's Parcel

An enormous parcel arrived for Jessie. It was delivered by special van. Her mum knew what was inside the parcel - but Jessica couldn't guess.

"You can open it up when you have tidied your room!" her mum told her.

The little girl looked glum. She hated tidying her room and didn't do it very often. That is why it looked such a mess!

At last Jessie finished and rushed to open her parcel.

"I'm so glad Mum made me tidy my room," said Jessie, "or there might not have been enough space for my playhouse!"

12 Patsy's Mobile

Patsy's little brother was a nuisance in the car. He hated sitting in his car seat, and he screamed when his seat belt was fastened. Sometimes he kept screaming until they reached the journey's end!

So before his next car ride, Patsy chose some of his favourite small toys and made him a mobile.

Now on long car trips, Patsy's little brother laughs and plays and then falls fast asleep.

13 Belinda's Bargain

Belinda loved bargains. She went to every sale and sometimes came home with the strangest things.

"What on earth have you bought that for?" her friends would ask.

"Because it was a bargain!" replied Belinda very pleased with herself.

One very hot summer afternoon she went to the sales to buy an outfit for her holidays, and this is what she came back with.

"These are all my bargains," said Belinda with pride.

"But what good is that outfit when you're going to the seaside?!" laughed her friends.

14 The Runaway Beach Ball

The tide took Daisy rabbit's beach ball out to sea and she began to cry.

"Don't get upset," said her big brother Donald. "I'll go out in my rowing boat and bring it back."

Donald rowed very hard and soon reached the ball. Quickly he reached over the side to grab it.

"Hey that's my nose!" yelled a seal as he popped up by the side of the boat.

"Here's your beach ball!" Then he balanced the ball on the tip of his nose and tossed it back to Donald.

15 Tickled Toes

Minnie and Winnie had been playing all day on the beach. They built a beautiful sandcastle and decorated it with flags and shells.

Their mother brought lunch in a basket and a rug to sit on. But now the sun had gone behind a cloud and the cold breeze was blowing in from the sea.

"Time to go home," called their mother as she packed up the picnic basket.

"No!" shouted Minnie and Winnie. "We're not ready!" and they carried on collecting shells.

Then all at once a huge crab scampered by and tickled their bare toes.

"We're ready now!" screamed Minnie and Winnie with a fright.

"Good," said their mother. "Let's go home!"

16 Footprints In The Sand

Some of the sea creatures were rather worried, they had found a trail of huge webbed footprints in the sand.

"Perhaps it's a prehistoric monster walking along the seashore!" whispered Ollie Octopus quite dismayed.

"No doubt he's hungry and looking for a meal!" said a starfish shaking with fright.

"I don't think so!" laughed a crab. "There's a little boy walking along the beach in a new pair of flippers, so you can stop trembling, you silly creatures!"

17 Underwater Wally Makes A Mistake

Underwater Wally was exploring on the very bottom of the ocean. "Not much down here," he mumbled, "only a few rocks and a bit of seaweed."

Just then in the darkness he saw a familiar shape. "Great," cried Underwater Wally, "someone to play with!"

All day long the two raced and chased all over the ocean.

At last Underwater Wally rose to the surface. "Come on, let's take a look at you!" the whale shouted to his new friend.

What a shock for Underwater Wally. His friend wasn't another whale at all, but a submarine.

"Would you believe I've been playing hide and seek with a submarine?" chuckled Underwater Wally and swam off to tell the other whales.

18 Diving Dennis

Dennis was a deep-sea diver. He spent so much of his time underwater that many of the fishes became his friends, and some of them even played tricks on him!

Once, when he was swimming past a giant clam shell, it suddenly sprang open. And there, deep inside were two huge eyes that glowed in the dark!

"My goodness!" gasped Dennis as he fell back, "it must be a monster in there."

"Don't be scared," said a little fish blowing bubbles. "It's just my brother playing hide and seek! Did he give you a fright?"

19 Treasure Trove

When Dennis went deep-sea diving he loved collecting shells. He called them the treasure of the sea, and when he went home he arranged them on the shelves round his room. Dennis was very proud of his collection of shells and often showed them to his friends.

One day, as he was exploring the ocean bed, he found a beautiful shell, the finest he had ever seen.

"What a treasure!" he said to himself as he took a closer look.

Somehow I think his fishy friends want to show him the treasures they have found!

20 Sea Stars

"I wish we could see the stars at night," said some of the sea creatures.

"They sound so beautiful," said a hermit crab.

"Indeed they are!" chorused the jellyfish. "We can see the stars when we float on top of the waves."

"They're quite right," said the dolphins. "We'll swim to the surface then come back and tell you about them."

"There's no need," said a baby squid, "for we have our very own stars!"

...And there were the starfish swimming around in the water, looking just like real stars in the sky.

21 Blowing Bubbles

It was Tom's unlucky day. Quite by accident he had upset a jug of orange juice. It wasn't his fault of course!

There he was helping to tidy the kitchen, and as he opened the fridge door, all the eggs fell out onto the floor. It wasn't his fault of course!

Somehow he managed to drop coffee grounds into the knife drawer and how did that blob of jam get underneath his shoe?

"Tom," said his mother with a deep sigh. "How would you like to blow bubbles? That's perfectly harmless!" and she closed the kitchen door.

So the rest of that morning Tom blew such wonderful bubbles - but he blew them through the keyhole and they floated all over the house and burst with a splat!

22 Knock! Knock! Who's There?

How do you know when a tortoise is at home? Tim the Tortoise's friends could never tell! Whenever he stuck his head inside his thick hard shell - he couldn't hear a thing!

So when someone came visiting, they would knock loudly on his back and get no reply.

One day somebody solved the problem. Now Tim the Tortoise hears every single one of his visitors.

23 Vera The Viper

Vera the Viper was very vain, she could not pass a mirror without admiring her reflection.

"One day Vera," hissed her father, "you will crack the glass!" But Vera didn't mind, she just loved looking at herself.

"I'm so pretty, oh so pretty!" she sang as she slithered along.

One summer afternoon she was gliding through the grass, preening herself in her looking glass, when she spied a fairground. "*The Hall Of Mirrors* looks exciting," said Vera. So she slipped inside.

Was she in for a shock! When poor Vera looked in the funny mirrors, she could hardly believe her eyes. "I'm so fat! I'm too thin! I look a freak!"

And from that day to this, Vera never looked in a mirror again.

24 What A Lot Of Hot Air

The coffee pot and the teapot were having a very heated argument at breakfast time.

"I'm much better than you!" hissed the boiling hot coffee pot, blowing steam from under his lid.

"Rubbish!" snapped the teapot. "People love tea and people love me. You're full of hot air, so there!" and she danced around the table and stuck out her tongue at the bad tempered coffee pot.

Along came a china cup and saucer. "Be quiet you two old windbags!" she cried. "Folks want coffee and folks want tea - and both of you are no good without me!"

25 Tibby Takes A Trip

Les the lighthouse keeper had lost his cat.

"I can't find Tibby at all," he told Snowy the Seagull. "I've looked everywhere!"

"I'll see what I can do," called Snowy as he took off and flew over the lighthouse.

Soon Snowy was back, he shook his head. "No sign of Tibby anywhere!"

Then Snowy gazed far out to sea. "Has a boat called here today?"

"Certainly!" said Les. "It came to bring my supplies for the week."

Snowy flapped his wings and went after the speeding boat.

As he flew down onto the deck, he spied Tibby asleep on a box of fish. The captain agreed to look after Tibby until he returned to the lighthouse in a weeks time.

Snowy sped of straight away to let Les the lighthouse keeper know that Tibby was safe and sound.

Cheer Up Trudi!

Trudi had a blue and red bike, she was very proud of it. One fine morning she rode her bike too near a brick wall and she fell off.

Sad to say she grazed both her knees and her elbows, she even had a cut on her forehead.

Poor Trudi ended up covered in plasters. When her dad saw what she had done he took his pen from his pocket and said, "Cheer up Trudi, and smile please!"

The Favourite Chair

Children always looked forward to visiting their Uncle Bengy's house, he had great tales to tell and made wonderful jam doughnuts dusted with sugar.

One day when the children went to see him, they opened the kitchen door, but instead of walking straight inside, they stopped to take a look around.

"There's something different," said one little boy.

"Where is our favourite chair?" cried another. "It's gone from the corner",

"I've thrown it out!" laughed Uncle Bengy. "I've bought a brand sparkling new one. Come and try it for size."

The children crowded onto the new chair. "It's horrid and very uncomfortable!"

The new chair gave a creak and a crack and all the children fell onto the floor.

"Well!" grinned Uncle Bengy, "I'd better bring your favourite chair back, lucky I didn't throw it on the bonfire!"

28 A Bed For The Night

One summer day the zoo keeper had to go away on business for a whole day and night.

Norah, the zoo keeper's wife, together with all the animals, waved him off at the zoo gates.

But when Norah came to look around, she found that the zoo keeper had taken the keys.

"Where will we all sleep tonight?" asked the animals.

"Don't worry!" shouted Norah. "It's summertime, tonight will be warm and we can all sleep outside."

But some of the smaller animals didn't like the idea of sleeping on the grass at all.

"It's alright!" said Norah, "I'll make sure that you have a comfortable bed tonight."

All that day she sat knitting in the warm sun. She used her thickest wool and an enormous pair of needles, and by bedtime she was all finished.

"It's getting late!" said Norah as the animals gathered round her. Then she tucked the little ones into their brand new comfortable hammocks.

29 Clever Gerald

Gerald thought he was very clever. "Do you know?" he said one day to his little sister Anne. "I can read my book upside down. Aren't I clever?"

Now Anne was just learning to read and found it very hard indeed. But she thought for a while and came up with an answer.

I think Anne knows how to read her book upside down as well as her clever brother Gerald, don't you?

30 The Clowns' Carpet

When the circus moved from town to town, everyone had to lend a hand to pack up the big top. Then the circus folk set out all the chairs round the ring, ready for people to sit on when they came to see the show.

It was the clowns' job to lay the long red carpet between the seats.

Now the clowns grew tired of carrying this heavy carpet every time the circus moved, so they thought of this bright idea and it worked perfectly every time!

31 Hunt The Thimble

One fine summer's evening when the visitors to the zoo had gone home, the zoo keeper and his wife Norah liked nothing better than to play Hunt The Thimble with the animals.

Everybody joined in and had a wonderful time - all except the parrots!

Before the game began, Norah would cover up the cage. "Sorry!" she said as she drew the curtains. "We can't have you giving the game away!"

Each time Hunt The Thimble was played the noisy parrots would squawk, "The thimble is in the eagle's nest, it's under the panda's water pot...there it is, in the gorilla's bunch of bananas!"

So that is why Norah always covers the parrots when Hunt The Thimble is being played.

The Teddy Bears Go To The Seaside

1

Pippa had never been to the seaside before. "You will need a bathing costume!" the other teddies told her.

So Pippa got out a photograph of her Great Aunt Araminta on the beach many years ago.

"I want a costume just like that!" said Pippa. "It looks very smart."

When Pippa got to the beach and changed into her costume, the other teddies couldn't stop laughing.

"Oh dear!" cried Pippa "I seem to be wearing the wrong clothes!"

The Teddies' Sandcastle

2

The teddies started to make a sandcastle.

"If we all help, ours could be the biggest one on the beach!"

So the teddies worked hard all morning, digging sand and building the giant castle, but by lunchtime it had fallen down.

"Never mind," said one of the teddies. "We'll try again, but this time we'll build something quite different."

Their sandteddy was so good it won first prize and all the teddies had a giant ice cream as a reward!

3 The Teddies Go Fishing

"Let's go fishing from the pier!" said one of the teddies.

"Can we come too?" asked the girls.

"If you can keep very still and quiet," replied the boys.

So two of the teddies hired rods and lines and set off for the pier.

"Do you know how to fish?" asked one of the teddies.

"Like this!" said the other as he cast out his line.

I don't think the girls are keeping very quiet now, do you?

4 Racing Teddies

Two of the teddies thought they would have a race along the promenade. One wore roller skates, the other had a skateboard.

"We're so fast!" they yelled as they sped along. "Nothing can catch us!"

Then to their amazement something whizzed past them at top speed...It was the girls on their new scooter, waving and grinning as they passed by!

5 Punch And Judy

It was a lovely sunny afternoon on the beach and everyone was waiting for the Punch and Judy show to begin. But where was the Punch and Judy man?

"Perhaps he's not coming today," said someone in the crowd and everyone looked very disappointed.

Nobody noticed some of the teddies slip quietly from their seats at the front.

All of a sudden the curtains of the Punch and Judy opened and the show began.

6 The Swimming Spoons

The Wooden Spoon people went for a holiday by the sea. They played on the beach, they dug in the sand and some days they sunbathed.

"I wished we could go in the sea," said one of the spoons, "but none of us can swim!"

"Don't forget," said another spoon, "we are wooden spoons, we can all float!"

7 Don And His Dumper Truck

Don and his dumper truck worked hard all day making new roads. It was hard, dusty, noisy work and very boring.

"We both need a holiday!" said Don to his dumper truck one day.

At that moment up came the foreman. "You're both needed at Sandy Bay. A high tide has washed so much sand onto the beach, it needs levelling."

So that is how Don and his dumper truck spent the summer months shifting soft sand and sunbathing on the beach. In fact, enjoying a really long holiday.

8 Dad's New Hosepipe

It was a very hot summer day and the children were playing out in the garden. All at once they rushed inside to find umbrellas and wellington boots.

"It can't be raining," said their mother as she looked out of the window. "The weather forecast is fine and sunny all day."

"It's not raining at all," cried the children as they ran outside. "Dad's using his new hosepipe!"

9 Iggy's Yacht

Iggy Frog and his friend Silver Minnow were busy watching a little girl and her father sailing their model yacht on the pond.

"How I wish I had a yatch with a red sail just like that one," said Iggy with a sigh.

That night when the little girl went home she forgot her yacht and left it behind in the reeds.

"Can I keep the yacht for my very own?" Iggy Frog asked Silver Minnow.

"Definitely not!" snapped the little fish. "She may come back for it tomorrow."

The little girl did not come back for it the next day, or the next, but when she did, she was carrying another yacht.

"She's forgotten all about her other boat," cried Silver Minnow. "I'm sure you can keep it now Iggy!"

10 Silly Iggy Frog

"I must varnish my boat!" said Iggy Frog as he jumped into the river with his paintbrush and tried to varnish his boat under water.

"Silly Iggy!" laughed his friend Silver Minnow. "First you have to pull your boat out of the water, turn it upside down, then you give it a coat of varnish!"

11 Marianne Wants A Pony

In summer, Marianne went for a holiday in the country. She stayed on a farm, and every day she rode on a Shetland pony that lived in a field at the back of the farmhouse.

At last the holiday came to an end and sadly Marianne had to say goodbye to the little pony.

'I do wish I could have a pony of my own,' thought Marianne on the journey home, but she knew it was impossible because she lived in a flat in the middle of a big city.

One day when Marianne came home from school she found a large packing case in the middle of the hall.

Can you guess what was inside?...A huge rocking horse with a flowing mane and a long tail.

"In a couple of years we are going to live in the country," said her dad. "Then you can have a real pony."

"Until then," cried Marianne, "my new rocking horse is just perfect!"

 ## Lazy Ludo

Ludo the lizard was very, very lazy. All year round he slept in the sun, except for two weeks when he went on holiday.

"I need a rest!" said Ludo as he went water-skiing and swimming and wind-surfing. "I need a rest from being lazy!"

Frederick's Frame

It was Frederick's first holiday by the sea. Every day the sun shone, he played on the beach. The sand was soft and warm and stuck between his toes, and the sea tasted very salty.

On the last day of Frederick's holiday, his mother took his photograph, and he collected a bucketful of seashells.

When Frederick got home he missed the sand and sea so much. His mother took out the photograph she had taken and showed Frederick how to make a very special frame for it. Then he put it in his bedroom to remind him of his very first holiday by the sea.

Blot And Buttercup

Blot the Dalmatian puppy was covered in black spots, they looked like splodges of ink.

His friend the retriever puppy had a yellow coat, and that is why she was known as Buttercup.

One day when Blot and Buttercup were sitting side by side on the path, a boy sped past on his bicycle. He rode through a puddle and splashed mud all over Buttercup.

"Now I look just like you!" Buttercup laughed as she looked across at Blot.

A Tight Squeeze

Gordon trapped his finger and had to go to hospital.

When the ambulance came to take him, Gordon was far too big to fit in! So the ambulance man had to slide back the roof and open the windows.

Now Gordon fits in perfectly, although it's a tight squeeze!

 At The Zoo

The twins went on a visit to the zoo. Although it was summer, the weather was cold and wet. Instead of t-shirts and shorts, the boys had to wear coats and boots.

"When you're dressed like that," laughed their Dad, "I can hardly tell you from the penguins!"

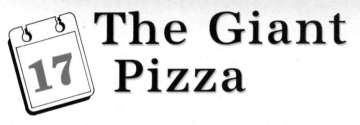 The Giant Pizza

One day three busy cooks had nothing whatsoever to do.

"Let's make something just for ourselves!" said the first cook.

"Why don't we make the biggest pizza in the world?" suggested the second.

"We'll start straight away!" cried the third.

It took the three cooks all morning to make and bake the biggest pizza you have ever seen.

"What are we going to do with it?" cried all three cooks. "We'll never eat it all ourselves!"

So they carried their giant pizza into town and everyone had a slice.

"Three cheers for the three busy cooks!" people shouted. "When are you going to make some more?"

18 Prudence Finds A Friend

Prudence Panda was sitting munching bamboo shoots in a lonely part of the forest.

Suddenly she heard a twig snap. "Help!" cried Prudence. "I hope it's not a savage monster that is going to eat me!"

Then she heard a voice say, "Don't eat me you savage monster!" and a head poked through the undergrowth - it was another panda.

"I thought you were a monster," Prudence laughed with relief.

"I thought you were a monster too," giggled the other panda. "Now we've met, let's be friends!"

19 Don't Shake Hands

Two dolphins met a giant squid.

"Don't speak to him!" said one of the dolphins.

"Is he dangerous?" asked the other.

"Not at all, but if he wants to shake hands, we'll be here all day!"

So the two dolphins swam away at top speed!

20 Carlo's Laces

Carlo practised for ages until he could tie his shoe laces. Day after day he put his shoes on the table and tied and untied his laces. He must have done it over a hundred times.

"Right!" said Carlo putting his shoes on the floor. "Today I shall put them on my feet, tie my laces and go to school."

Silly Carlo! He's tied his shoe laces together. He hasn't quite got the hang of it yet, has he?

21 Moving House

The Brown family were moving house. The children put their toys in a huge packing crate and the removal men lifted it onto the van with the rest of the furniture. Then they closed the doors and set off for the Brown's new home.

As soon as they arrived, the removal men unpacked the crates. When they were finished, they had a cup of tea. They were just about to drive off, when they heard a noise like a siren - it came from inside the van!

They took a look inside, and there was the crate of toys, quite forgotten. When the toys had realised they had been left behind, Teddy sounded the siren on the toy fire engine as loudly as he could...and thank goodness someone heard!

22 Grapefruit For Breakfast

Minnie and Winnie had cereal every day for breakfast before they went to school.

On Saturday mornings they had more time, so they ate half a juicy grapefruit each, with toast to follow.

That is why both girls are wearing sunglasses indoors!

23 Rabbit Stew

Very early one bright morning, Mr. Fox went into his garden to pick vegetables.

"I need carrots, onions, a couple of parsnips and a bunch of herbs," he said out loud. "Today I'm going to catch a rabbit and make myself a tasty rabbit stew!"

Now Reggie Rabbit overheard Mr. Fox early that bright morning and decided to teach him a lesson.

After breakfast Mr. Fox crept quietly down the lane looking for a plump tasty rabbit to put in his stew. But who should be behind the hedge but Reggie and his friends, just waiting to teach Mr. Fox a lesson.

As Mr. Fox came near, the rabbits stood on each others shoulders and appeared from behind the hedge.

"Would you like to put me in your stew?" bellowed Reggie in his loudest voice.

Poor Mr. Fox saw the giant rabbit and ran for his life.

"I don't think he'll go hunting rabbits again for a very long time!" laughed the rabbits as they jumped down.

24 The Jigsaw Piece That Ran Away

Once upon a time there was a jigsaw in a box on the top shelf of a cupboard.

"It's very boring in here," said one of the pieces. "I'm going to run away!"

So the jigsaw piece jumped out of the box and ran through the front door into the street outside. Straight away a big foot trod on him, then a bicycle ran over him. But worse of all, a dog picked him up in his mouth and tried to bury him in the ground.

Then a man digging the garden picked him up. "Oh, its just a bit of an old puzzle!" and he threw the jigsaw piece over the hedge back into the street.

"How silly I am," the jigsaw piece cried. "How I miss my box and the rest of the jigsaw."

When at last he found his way home and got back into the box, the other pieces of the jigsaw were delighted to see him.

"You're no good without us, and we're no use without you!" they said one to another.

Later that day a little boy took down the box and looked inside. "What a smashing jigsaw, I shall play with this all day long!" And he did.

25 Billy The Goat

When visitors came to the farm, the farmer and his wife always made sure that Billy the goat was tied up.

"It's not fair!" muttered the other animals, and one of them untied him.

"I wish you hadn't done that," shrieked the farmer's wife. "Now we shall never get any visitors!"

26 The Thirsty Fieldmice

One hot afternoon the fieldmice found a can of fizzy drink left behind by some picnickers.

"Who would like a cool drink?" asked Monty, one of the mice.

"We would!" cried the rest, "but we don't know how?"

"Easy!" cried Monty and he rushed off to find some hollow grass stalks.

Then the fieldmice climbed up to the top of the can and drank the fizzy drink down to the last drop!

27 The Cow Jumped Over The Moon

One day the farm cat told the little brown cow a nursery rhyme.

"Hey diddle diddle, the Cat and the Fiddle, the Cow jumped over the Moon!"

The little brown cow listened very carefully. "How I wish I could jump over the moon, like the cow in the nursery rhyme."

"You'll never be able to do that!" laughed the farm cat, and he strolled off to sleep in the sun.

But the farm cat was wrong! That night when the moon was high in the sky, the little brown cow saw its reflection shining in a big puddle in the middle of the farmyard.

Before the moon could disappear, the little brown cow galloped across the yard and jumped over the puddle.

"I've jumped over the moon, like the cow in the nursery rhyme!" she cried with delight, and the farm cat had to agree!

28 Aunt Chloe Comes To Tea

When Aunt Chloe came to tea everyone promised to be on their best behaviour.

"I love trifle!" chuckled Aunt Chloe and gobbled up the lot.

"Chocolate eclairs are my favourite!" she exclaimed and ate every one.

"These cream cakes are delicious!" Aunt Chloe went on, and emptied the plate in a trice.

"Pass me those currant buns with icing on top!" she shouted, pushing back her chair.

"I think the currants look like dead flies!" said one of the children.

"How revolting!" gasped Aunt Chloe, and she ran from the table.

"Great!" cried the children. "We love iced currant buns, they're our favourite!"

Quickly they tucked into a large plateful, because that was all that was left.

29 Telling The Time

"What time is it?" buzzed the bees as they flew around the garden.

"I wish we knew!" sang the sparrows on the blackcurrant bushes.

"Does anyone have a watch?" asked a yellow butterfly.

"Don't be so silly!" snapped the dragonfly. "We're all far too small to wear a watch!" And everybody laughed.

Then one day a sundial was set up in the garden. Now all the birds and insects that fly around can see exactly what time it is!

30 Up In A Balloon

The birds had been to a party and now it was time to fly home.

"Race you!" the big birds called to the smaller ones.

"That's not fair!" the little birds called back. "Our wings are so small, we can't fly as fast as you."

Now the little birds had each been given a balloon to take home from the party. All of a sudden a strong gust of wind lifted them high into the air and blew them all the way home.

"We're the winners!" sang the little birds when the big birds reached home at last.

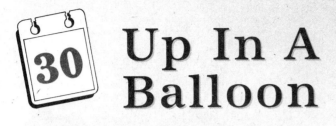

31 The Old Curtains

Mrs. Jones bought lots of material and made new curtains for all her windows.

"Can we have the old ones?" her children asked.

"Whatever for?" said Mrs. Jones surprised. "The colours have faded and they look really shabby."

"Don't worry," said the children. "We are going to make good use of them.

The next few days the children were so busy, Mrs. Jones only saw them at meal times.

"Come and look at the bottom of the garden!" chorused the children. And when Mrs. Jones went to look, she hardly recognised her shabby curtains!

1 Cloth Monkey's New Toy

"I wish I had something to play with," sighed the cloth monkey. "The dolls have their dolls' house, the other toys can play with bricks and skittles or ride on trains, but I want something of my very own to play with!"

Next day, when the toys were taken out into the garden, they tried to think of something that the cloth monkey would really enjoy.

Suddenly, one of the toys thought of a clever idea, then whispered the plan to the others.

Quickly, the toys set to work. They took the broom handle and sawed it into six pieces. Then they found the washing line and cut and measured it very carefully. In next to no time, the toys had made the cloth monkey a rope ladder of his very own!

2 The Lonely Bluebird

The little bluebird was feeling so lonely. He had no-one to chirp to and no friends to fly around with. Sadly, he perched on a windowsill near to his favourite tree.

A little girl, who was just finishing her breakfast, saw the unhappy little bluebird and called her mother. "Is anything wrong with that poor bluebird?" she asked.

"Nothing at all," smiled her mother. "I know just the right way to cheer him up, and you can help me!"

Quickly they searched the kitchen cupboards for nuts, seeds and all the things birds like to eat. Then they hung them up in the tree next to the kitchen window.

Soon the garden was full of hungry birds. The little bluebird found plenty of friends and never felt lonely again.

3 Good Night Sammy Squirrel

Sammy the little red squirrel was afraid of the dark. "I like going to bed," Sammy told his mother, "but I don't like it when you switch off the light!"

"I think I know some friends of mine who can help," smiled Mother Squirrel.

That night, when Sammy went to bed, his mother tapped on the bedroom window. Soon lots of tiny lights appeared in the darkness outside.

It was the firefly family! They flew around the little squirrel's bedroom window every night until he fell fast asleep.

4 Gathering Nuts

Every afternoon, a group of friends went into the woods to help the squirrels gather nuts.

"I don't like this job at all!" cried one of the rabbits as a shower of nuts fell down onto his head.

"I bet that hurt," giggled Tim Turtle, whose head was protected by his hard shell.

This made the animals think. They all rushed home and soon came back dressed in just the right hats for gathering nuts!

5 The First Day At School

One of the little grey rabbits was very excited. It was his first day at school.

He got up very early and put on his new uniform.

"My, how smart you look!" said his mother as they set off for school.

When the other small animals crowded round to meet the little grey rabbit, they all began to giggle.

"Look down at your feet," laughed a small hedgehog, "you've come to school in odd socks!"

Mrs. Rabbit looked dismayed. "I hope he's not going to cry," she whispered to the teacher.

Instead the little grey rabbit took a deep breath and said, "Yes I know I'm wearing odd socks. In fact I have another pair exactly like them at home!"

6 Inside A Log

Blot and Buttercup were playing in the wood. They were having a wonderful time racing and chasing through the autumn leaves. All of a sudden Blot spied a hollow log, he squeezed inside to hide from Buttercup.

"I love hide and seek!" barked Buttercup, and she followed Blot into the hollow logs.

An owl who perched on a branch nearby shook his head, "I've never seen a dog with a spotted head and a yellow tail before," and he flew off looking very puzzled!

7 Ludo's Buried Treasure

Ludo the lizard's garden needed digging, but he was far too lazy to do it himself. So one day he went out and bought lots of tiny toys and gifts, then he buried them all over his garden.

He put a notice on his garden gate which read, 'Come and dig for treasure'.

Soon Ludo's garden was full of animals all digging furiously. Ludo, you lazy lizard, you've managed to get out of digging your garden once more!

8 Willy And The Grasshopper

When Willy the worm poked his head through the soil one day, he came face to face with a grasshopper.

Willy watched him hop around for a while until he felt quite dizzy.

"Tell me grasshopper," asked Willy, "how did you learn to jump so high?"

"I do one hundred skips every morning," said the grasshopper, and he showed Willy how.

"I think I'll stick to wriggling," sighed Willy, and he popped back down his worm hole.

Grandpa's Tree

9

Grandpa planted a tree in his garden. He came outside to look at it every day. In spring it had soft green leaves, and in early summer it was covered with pale pink blossom.

"I wish I had a photograph of my tree!" said Grandpa, "but everyone was far too busy and forgot to take one!"

When autumn came, the leaves on the tree turned red and yellow. It looked beautiful.

"Now's the time to take a photograph of my tree," Grandpa reminded everyone.

"We'll do it tomorrow!" the family promised. But when at last, someone went outside to take the picture, all the leaves had fallen off!

"Poor Grandpa!" everyone said. "We should have taken the picture when we promised and now the tree is bare."

So they set to work and tied the leaves back on the branches one by one. Then someone took the photograph and Grandpa never noticed!

Hats Off

10

A strong north wind was blowing. It whistled through the woods, it bent the branches on the trees and scattered dry leaves all over the place.

Everyone out walking in the woods that morning lost their hats. The north wind twirled them round and round, blew them high into the air, and let them fall.

Now everyone is trying to find their own hat before the wind blows them off again!

11 Fizzy Grizzly And The Fence

Fizzy Grizzly's gran asked him to paint her fence.

"Certainly Gran," said Fizzy Grizzly. "Do you mind if I have a can of my favourite drink before I start!"

So Gran fetched the drink straight away, and Fizzy Grizzly leaned on the fence while he drank it.

All of a sudden there was a creak and a groan and the whole fence fell down.

"Never mind," laughed Gran. "Forget that old fence, we'll plant a hedge instead."

12 Stop The Train

Gordon went to the railway station and bought a ticket to Forest Town.

"I'm sorry!" said the station master. "No trains stop at this station today. Not even if I wave my red flag!"

"Don't bother waving your flag," said Gordon. "I'll make sure the train stops here today!"

13 Dora Comes To Stay

One day Dora the dormouse came from the town to stay with her cousin Dottie in the country.

That night when she went to bed, Dora got the shock of her life when she looked out of the window.

"Help! Help!" she screamed as she ran downstairs to find Dottie.

"There's an upside down mouse looking in at the window."

"It's only Matt the Bat," laughed Dottie. "He's a good friend of mine, come along and meet him. He's great fun!"

14 Dora The Snorer

Next morning when Dora woke up, Matt the Bat had flown away.

"He sleeps during the day," explained cousin Dottie.

"And I think all the folk around here will be sleeping in the day too...Dora! You're such a snorer!"

"Sorry!" Dora blushed. "I forgot to tell you about that!"

15 Quiet Please

"I never knew that it was so noisy in the countryside!" said Dora. "All day long there are bees buzzing, frog croaking, birds cheeping, cocks crowing in the morning, and owls hooting all night long. The town is much quieter."

"You need a pair of ear muffs," chuckled Dottie, "to wear until you go home!"

Iggy's Idea

16

Iggy Frog had heard Dora's snores right down by the stream.

"Would you like to sleep aboard my raft moored by the bank side?" Iggy asked.

"What a splendid idea," cried Dora. "But I ought to warn you that the rocking of the raft will make me sleep soundly and I might snore louder than ever!"

Goodbye Dora

17

It was time for Dora to go back home to town.

"What are you doing upside down?" asked her cousin Dottie.

"Just saying goodbye to my new friend Matt the Bat!" smiled Dora.

18 Fenella Flies Away

Tiny Fenella Fieldmouse was holding on tightly to her balloon when a strong gust of wind blew her high into the air.

Quickly her friends below made paper darts to pop the balloon before it floated away, and two of them made sure she had a soft landing!

19

Keeping Fit

The hare and the tortoise decided to keep fit.

"Shall we go jogging?" asked the hare.

"This is the only way I can keep up with you!" laughed the tortoise.

20 Sam The Spider

"Why is everybody frightened of me?" asked Sam the spider as he dropped down from the ceiling and scurried across the floor. "I'm just an ordinary big black spider!"

Strange to say, no-one answered, they just screamed and ran away.

One day Sam had a wonderful idea. He went shopping and bought three pairs of leggings and a sweater. Now nobody runs away from Sam - because who is afraid of a pink and white spider?

21 Mr. Fox's Trap

One day when Mr. Fox was walking through the wood, he thought of a marvellous idea for catching rabbits.

"I shall dig a deep hole, and cover it up with leaves and branches," he sniggered to himself. "When those rabbits come scampering through the wood, they won't see the hole, they'll fall in, then I shall eat them for my dinner!"

So sly Mr. Fox dug his hole, covered it with branches and sat down to wait.

"I think I need a few more branches!" said Mr. Fox. So straight away he climbed up the tree and began sawing.

Somehow I think Mr. Fox is going to be caught in his own trap, don't you?

22 Pierre's Accordion

One day Pierre lost his accordion and people couldn't sing and dance to his music.

"I can't find it," said Pierre shaking his head.

"Are you sure you've looked everywhere?" said his wife as she sat down on the sofa beside him.

"What's that dreadful noise?" cried Pierre's wife as she jumped up.

"You've found my lost accordion," laughed Pierre. "It was under the cushion and you sat on it!"

23 The Painted Door

One morning Angelo and Lorenzo were cleaning out their garden shed.

Angelo threw some old tins outside, the lids fell off and paint splashed all down the shed door.

Lorenzo thought this was great fun and threw some more, and very soon the shed door was covered in paint of every colour - and so were Lorenzo and Angelo!

A man walking by stopped to admire their work. "Can I buy your shed door to hang in my art gallery?" he said and gave them lots of money.

Lorenzo and Angelo could hardly believe their luck!

24 The New Car

Next day Lorenzo and Angelo went to buy a car with all their money.

"I want a shiny limousine!" said Lorenzo.

"I prefer a fast racing car!" said Angelo and they began to argue.

The man at the garage counted up all their money, then he went into the showroom and brought out a car.

"You have just enough money to buy this!" the man beamed.

"That will do nicely!" said Angelo and Lorenzo together.

So they packed all their luggage into the back and went on their holidays.

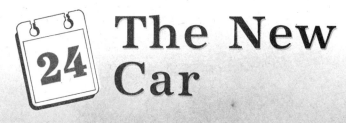

25 A Surprise For Pedro

Pedro the parrot was puzzled, he kept finding brightly coloured feathers all over the house especially near the cupboard under the stairs.

"There must be another parrot living here!" squawked Pedro.

So the first time the door of the cupboard door under the stairs was left open, Pedro took a look inside. Was he in for a surprise!

"It's only a feather duster," squawked Pedro, "There's no parrot at all. Silly me!"

26 The Old Van

"This farmyard is very untidy!" announced the farmer one day as he looked around. "It's full of broken gates and rusty old ploughs that are no good at all."

"It's high time we cleared up!" the farmer's wife agreed.

"First we'll have to get rid of this broken down old van," said the farmer. "Send for Tessa and her breakdown truck!"

When Tessa arrived, she hooked up the wrecked van to her truck.

"Are you taking it to the scrapyard?" asked the animals.

"Wait and see!" said Tessa with a smile.

27 The New Camper

The next afternoon Tessa returned to the farm and she wasn't in her breakdown truck. This time she was driving a bright yellow camper.

"I wish we had one of those," sighed the animals as they crowed round, "then we could go camping once in a while!"

"Don't you recognise your old wrecked van?" laughed Tessa. "I repaired it last night and sprayed it yellow. It's all yours now!"

28 Pull Down The Blind

"I don't like dark nights!" said Veronica. "I miss looking out of my window into the garden."

"The dark nights last for a long time, right until spring," said her mother. "I'll have to see what I can do!"

Now when Veronica pulls down her blind, she is quite happy.

29 Belinda Picks Pears

Belinda the ragdoll and the rest of the toys were picking pears from the tree in their garden.

"The biggest ones are right at the top," cried Belinda, "I'll climb up and get them."

But when she reached the top, Belinda realised she couldn't get down.

"Help!" screamed Belinda "Get me down at once!"

"We can't," cried the other toys. "You're too far up."

Quickly the clown ran indoors and fetched a skipping rope. Then he shouted to two crows sitting in the pear tree and asked them, very politely, if they would rescue Belinda.

And this is how they did it!

Soon Belinda was back on the ground safe and sound.

"Give us all those big juicy pears as a reward!" the crows cawed. And Belinda had to agree.

30 The New Garage

Don and his dumper truck were kept busy all the autumn helping everyone to clear the fallen leaves. They worked hard from morning until night keeping the streets and parks tidy.

"Don and his dumper truck should have a reward for all their hard work!" announced the Town Mayor.

So everyone got together and built a special garage for the dumper truck.

"That will keep you warm and dry when the winter comes!" laughed Don as he parked his truck in the new garage.

Helen Finds A Secret Store

Helen the inquisitive hamster liked autumn. She liked the way the leaves changed colour and the rustling sound they made when she scurried through the woods.

Now Helen, being very inquisitive, rooted around in the fallen leaves, just in case someone had dropped something that she might find.

One day, as she was searching near the bottom of an oak tree, she looked up into the hollow of the trunk and found a store of nuts. Straight away Helen ran off to tell the first person she met, which happened to be a red squirrel.

"I'm so grateful!" the red squirrel cried throwing his arms round Helen. "I'd quite forgotten where I had hidden my secret store of nuts for the winter, and you have helped me find them!"

Thank You Helen!

The next day the red squirrel paid Helen the hamster a visit.

"I know you don't like nuts to eat!" said the squirrel as he handed Helen a prettily wrapped box.

"What's inside?" asked Helen, inquisitive as always.

"A thank you gift!" smiled the squirrel, for inside the box was a beautiful necklace made from nuts.

3 How Old Is Grandad?

It was Grandad's birthday, and Jake and his mother went to the baker's shop to buy a special cake.

"How old is Grandad?" asked Jake. "How many candles shall we put on his cake?"

"Grandad doesn't like anyone to know how old he really is!" laughed Jake's mother. "And I don't think you could get a cake big enough to hold all the candles!"

Then she winked.

"Put this on the top," said the lady in the shop, "that will keep everybody guessing!"

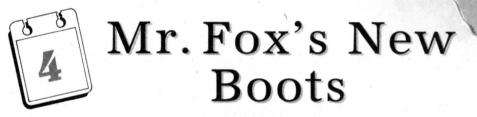

4 Mr. Fox's New Boots

Mr. Fox bought some new boots. "These are just right for chasing rabbits!" sniggered Mr. Fox as he put them on. "I shall run faster in these boots than ever before."

So off Mr. Fox ran to the rabbit's house, speeding along in his new boots.

Now when Mr. Fox reached the rabbit's garden gate, he saw a notice that read WET CEMENT. But he was running so fast in his new boots, he couldn't stop.

I think Mr. Fox is going to leave his new boots behind, don't you?

The Apple Orchard

5

Ma and Pa Bramley had an orchard. In it grew the crispest juiciest apples you ever tasted. This year the trees were full of apples just ready for picking.

"I'm afraid we're both getting too old to climb ladders and gather our apple harvest this year!" said Ma to Pa as they met the postman at the gate.

"It's a problem," said the postman shaking his head. "Perhaps I could come up with the answer over a cup of tea and a couple of your delicious scones. They always make me think better."

Ma and Pa Bramley sat around the table with the postman (who ate five scones!).

"Must dash!" cried the postman as he brushed the crumbs from his uniform. "I'll have your problem solved by tomorrow!"

The Missing Apples

6

The next morning when Ma and Pa Bramley got up and looked out of the bedroom window they were in for a shock. The apple trees were empty.

"I can't see any ladders," said Pa, "but someone has pinched all the apples!"

"Perhaps apple thieves have stolen all our fruit!" cried Ma.

"I must be dreaming," gasped Pa, "I've just seen somebody walk past our bedroom window!"

Ma and Pa were not dreaming. When they looked again, they saw who had pinched all the fruit. A man who walked on stilts and two jugglers had come from the circus nearby and picked all Ma and Pa's apples for them in no time at all.

7 Apple Pies

After all the apples had been picked and stored in the barn, Ma and Pa thought of a wonderful way to thank all the folks that had helped them.

They baked pies! Lots and lots of apple pies for everyone to eat and enjoy.

"To thank you all," said Ma Bramley, "we will bake pies for you all every week until next apple picking time."

8 Pippin The Pig

Pippin was Ma and Pa Bramley's pet pig. She lived in their orchard and liked nothing better than grabbing fallen apples.

One day Pippin found the biggest apple she had ever seen. "This is mine!" squealed the little pink pig. "I shall eat every bit myself!" So straight away she took a great big bite. Poor Pippin, someone had found the apple before she did!

OCTOBER

9 The Scarecrow Contest

During the second week in October, the town where Heidi lived held a Scarecrow Festival. A beautiful silver cup was given to the person who made the finest scarecrow.

Now Heidi knew she could win the prize if she tried hard enough. So she collected some old clothes and a floppy straw hat and began to make her scarecrow.

First she stuffed the trousers and was halfway through the jacket when she ran out of straw.

"Not to worry!" Heidi laughed. "I'll dress myself up and enter the contest."

Heidi stood perfectly still with the other scarecrows until the judge said, "Here is the winner!"

As he pinned the badge on her ragged coat, Heidi jumped for joy.

The judge got such a surprise. "I don't think we've ever had a straw-woman win our contest before."

10 A Dish Fit For A Pig

Pippin the little pink piglet lived with Ma and Pa Bramley.

One day while they were walking through the orchard, Pippin came to a decision. "I'm too fine a pig to eat my dinner from a trough or a bucket!" she announced. "I want a special plate of my own!"

Ma and Pa Bramley searched the shops and stores for a dish fit for Pippin, but they had no luck.

Now a little way up the lane from Ma and Pa's orchard lived a potter. She heard what Pippin wanted, so she made a dish fit for a princess - or a little pink piglet!

11 A Shock For Sammy

Sammy Squirrel was always reading about monsters and giants and all sorts of scary things.

One windy day as he was reading in his room at the top of his tall tree, a huge monster's face appeared right outside the window.

Poor Sammy got such a fright, he jumped inside a cupboard to hide.

Don't be frightened Sammy! It's a great day for flying kites and Mr. Badger is flying his new one right outside your window!

12 Surprise, Surprise Mr. Wolf

Mr. Wolf was always trying to get into the three pigs' new brick house - but with no luck!

"One day I shall get inside," Mr. Wolf sniggered, "then those three fat tender pigs will be mine!"

Now as he crept round the corner of the brick house, Mr. Wolf found that someone had left a ladder outside - how careless!

At once Mr. Wolf saw his chance and climbed up onto the roof.

"I'll go down the chimney and surprise them!" he sniggered.

Now it just so happened that the three little pigs had decided to sweep their chimney, and at the very moment Mr. Wolf reached the chimney pot, out popped the brush and covered him with soot.

It was the three little pigs' turn to surprise Mr. Wolf, don't you agree?

13 Fizzy Grizzly Cuts His Hedge

Fizzy Grizzly shook his money box. "It's not rattling," he sighed. "It must be empty!"

Next he looked in all his pockets and they were empty too!

"I shall have to find a job, then I can earn lots of money to buy my favourite fizzy drinks!" declared Fizzy Grizzly. "But first of all I must cut the hedge round my garden. It's grown so tall I can't see over the top."

So Fizzy Grizzly got out the steps and the shears and started work. He snipped and clipped all morning and by afternoon a crowd had gathered. Fizzy Grizzly had cut his hedge into lots of wonderful shapes.

"How very clever!" shouted somebody in the crowd and threw some money into Fizzy Grizzy's hat, which he had left on the ground.

Very soon everyone did the same, and soon Fizzy Grizzly had enough money to buy fizzy drinks for a long time.

14   Pedro Cleans The Car

Toby and Ted promised to clean Dad's car. Toby waxed and polished the paintwork until it shone and Ted cleaned the windows until they sparkled.

"Just a minute," cried Toby standing on tiptoe, "we haven't done the roof!"

"We can't reach," said Ted, "We're too small!"

So they went inside and fetched Pedro their pet parrot. He flew up onto the car roof with the wash leather in his beak, and very soon the car looked like new!

15   What A Squash!

Wendy said goodnight and went upstairs to bed.

After a little while she shouted to her mum and dad to come upstairs.

"Is anything the matter?" said her dad.

"Can't you sleep?" asked her mum.

"Perhaps she needs a drink of water," Dad went on.

"She might be frightened of the dark," said Mum.

This made Wendy laugh. "I called you upstairs to ask for a bigger bed, it's such a squash in here!"

16 The Cookie Tin

"I can smell cookies!" said one little chipmunk to the other.

"Chocolate chip cookies!" said the other.

And there in the long grass was a cookie tin.

"It's empty!" cried one little chipmunk as he looked inside.

"Never mind!" said the other. "It will make a perfect drum for us to play very loudly!"

17 One Way To Keep Quiet

The crocodile and the alligator were always arguing over who had the biggest jaws.

"I can eat a whole table full of food!" snapped the alligator.

"I once ate everything in the supermarket in one great gulp!" yelled the crocodile.

They argued so loudly that the other animals got fed up with both of them. Then one day somebody gave them a box of sticky toffee which stuck their jaws together...and that kept them quiet for a very long time!

18 Look Out, There's The Fox

It was getting dark, and all the hens were perching on the hen house roof.

"I wish they would come down," said the farmer's wife. "I must lock them up for the night or the fox might get them!"

All of a sudden a dark shape came through the farm gate.

"Look out, here's the fox!" squawked the hens. They flew off the hen house roof at once, and the farmer's wife shut the door when they were all safe inside. Then Bob the sheepdog trotted across the yard.

"Those silly hens thought that you were the fox," said the farmer's wife as she patted the dog. "That is why they came down from the hen house roof!"

19 Koala Phones Home

Every time Koala went on one of his long trips, he promised his mother that he would phone her twice a week.

He never forgot, but each time he picked up the phone, he couldn't remember the number!

He wrote it down on a piece of paper, but he lost it! He scribbled the number on his paw, but when he washed them, it disappeared!

The very next time he went away, his mother gave him a present that he could wear...now Koala will never forget to phone home!

20 Ella Fights A Fire

One afternoon when Ella the elephant was walking across the field where the circus was camped, she noticed a lot of smoke coming from behind the Big Top.

"Fire! Fire!" she shouted, then quickly filled her trunk with water from a tank nearby.

"Don't panic!" Ella cried, then trundled off as fast as she could to squirt water on the flames.

Oh dear! Ella has just put out the barbecue the circus folk were having after the show.

Never mind Ella, better safe than sorry!

21 The Fieldmice Take A Ride

"I wish we could go to the fair," said one of the fieldmice to the others.

"But we're far too small to go on any of the rides," said the youngest, looking very disappointed.

"If we could borrow Mrs. Hedgehog's big umbrella, we could make our own ride," suggested the eldest.

Now the fieldmice are happy - until it rains and Mrs. Hedgehog asks for her umbrella back!

22 Inside Mark's Pencil Case

One day the pencils in Mark's pencil case had an argument. The red pencil was sure that he was the brightest and best of all. The blues and greens were rowing with the oranges and yellows, and the purple pencil was yelling at everyone.

Then Mark reached inside his pencil case and drew a picture using all his colours.

At lunchtime he put them in the case, and the pencils started arguing all over again about who was best!

Then all at once from the corner of the pencil case came a tiny voice.

"None of you are any good without me!" It was a little silver pencil sharpener.

"When your points are blunt, none of you can draw again until I sharpen you. So I really think that I'm the best!" said the pencil sharpener with a grin.

23 The Little Blue Duck

The ducks on the duck pond were making a terrible din. The farmer and his wife were having breakfast and could hear the noise inside the house.

"I'd better see what all the fuss is about!" said the farmer's wife as she pulled on her wellington boots.

When she reached the pond she burst out laughing.

"Is this what the noise is all about?" And she knelt down and reached for the plastic duck her little boy played with in the bath every night.

"You silly ducks. It's just a toy!"

24 Baby Bear Leaves Home

Baby Bear decided to leave home and take a look at the world outside his garden. So he packed a pot of his very favourite honey and off he went.

When some of the older bears realised he was missing, they were very worried. "We must send out a search party to try and find him, he can't have gone very far!"

"I don't think there will be any need for that," smiled Mother Bear as she walked out of the garden gate. "Just follow the bees!"

A short walk down the lane they found Baby Bear. He had just opened the pot of his very favourite honey, and was sitting sharing it with the bees!

25 Baby Bett Brown

The Browns' baby, Bett, put everything into her mouth.

She chewed the bars of her cot and the back of her highchair. She nibbled her brother and sister's toys, and bit them if they came too close. Worst of all, she chewed their best books which made all the corners wet and soggy.

But Mother had the answer. She sewed Bett a rag book with pages of cloth instead of paper. Now everybody's happy, especially Bett!

26 Pedro's Sunflowers

On warm days Pedro the parrot liked to sit outside on his perch eating his favourite food - sunflower seeds.

Now Mr. Brown from next door didn't like Pedro, because he squawked and made too much noise when Mr. Brown wanted to sleep.

Pedro didn't like Mr. Brown either, because he poked his stick through the fence and tried to knock Pedro off his perch.

So whenever Pedro was eating sunflower seeds, he would spit a few over the fence into Mr. Brown's garden.

No wonder Mr. Brown looks puzzled. He'll never guess why his garden is full of giant sunflowers!

27 The Greens' Hobby

The Green children had a hobby - they collected things!

Dolly collected vegetables.

Molly collected fruit.

And Holly collected ice creams. Now isn't that a strange hobby!

They collected the magnets that stick onto the fridge...and here is Dolly, Molly and Holly's collection displayed in the Greens' kitchen!

28 Susie's Surprise

Susie planted sweetcorn seeds in the warm spring soil. By the time autumn came, they had grown into sweet, juicy cobs of corn. All the family loved eating fresh corn on the cob, and soon there were only a few cobs left.

"I shall be sorry when the sweetcorn is finished," said Susie to Aunt Maude, who had come from the country to stay.

"Give me the green husks from around the corn," smiled Aunt Maude, "and I will make you something to keep, that will remind you of your sweetcorn."

Very carefully, Aunt Maude dried the husks, and when they were stiff and crisp, she made them into a beautiful cornhusk doll!

29 Sweeping Leaves

"Does anyone like sweeping leaves?" asked a little grey rabbit one autumn day.

"NO!" cried the woodland folk altogether.

"It has to be done the same time every year," sighed the fox, "so we'd better get on with it!"

"But it's so boring!" cried everyone as they shuffled through the leaves that covered the woodland paths.

Trust Grey Badger to think of an excellent idea...Now everyone wants to sweep up the autumn leaves!

Surprise In A Shoe Box

30

It was Anna's birthday the day before Halloween. She always had a party and all her guests came dressed as witches.

"Would you like to do something different this year?" asked her mother.

"Oh no!" cried Anna. "Everyone loves dressing up as a witch."

So Anna's mother thought that *she* would do something different this year!

When all the guests had arrived and it was time for tea, Anna's mother gave everyone a shoe box. Inside were sandwiches, cakes and cookies and all kinds of party food.

All the children tucked in, but as they reached for the last treat in the box, each child gave a loud scream. Someone pulled out a big black hairy spider, then someone else found a bat with flappity wings. In one box was a rat, in another a lizard and a slimy toad - all rubber of course!

Soon the children were throwing them all over the place and popping them down each others' clothes.

And at the end of the party, the children took them home to frighten the life out of their mums and dads!

Trick Or Treat

31

One Halloween two little ghosts were chattering to one another as they walked through the woods.

"Are you afraid of anything?" one ghost asked the other.

"I'm not afraid of witches on broomsticks or big black spiders with hairy legs. I'm not afraid of owls that hoot in the dark, or spooky noises in the night. I'm only afraid of one thing!" whispered the little ghost as he looked seriously around him. "I'm scared stiff of all those children dressed up as ghosts and skeletons on Halloween - they make me tremble with fright!"

And with that the two little ghosts ran shrieking through the woods.

1 The Racing Pumpkin

On the day after Halloween two little chipmunks found a pumpkin.

"Shall we eat it?" asked one.

"I hate pumpkin," said the other. "It tastes awful!"

"Then let's live in it," said the first little chipmunk. "It would make a wonderful house!"

"It's far too small for both of us," laughed the second one. "But I know what we can do with it. Close your eyes and wait and see!"

2 New Jackets

The weather was beginning to turn cold. Some mornings when Blot and Buttercup went out for a walk, the air was frosty and the wind was chilly.

"Time for us to choose new jackets!" said Buttercup shivering.

So the next time they were taken to the pet shop, Blot and Buttercup chose the ones they liked the best.

Don't they look smart in their new jackets?

3 Buttons, Bows And Beads

Dolly liked buttons! Molly liked bows! And Holly liked beads!

It's very easy to tell which toy belongs to Dolly, which toy belongs to Molly and which toy belongs to Holly. Just match up the buttons, bows and beads!

4 Who Are You?

Minnie and Winnie went to a party. When it was time to go home, the two girls were each given a lucky bag and a huge balloon.

When they got home, Winnie rang the bell and Minnie knocked loudly on the door.

As Mum and Dad opened the door, they both gasped in surprise.

"Who are you?" asked Dad.

"I don't know you two!" chuckled Mum.

"It's Minnie and Winnie," yelled the two girls. "Let us in please!"

5 Fireworks At The Zoo

"Would you like a firework display tonight?" Norah the zoo keeper's wife asked the animals.

"Yes please!" yelled the smaller animals getting very excited.

The bigger animals looked worried. "We don't like fireworks!" growled the bear. "They make a loud bang and can be dangerous!"

"Don't worry," smiled Norah, "the zoo keeper has thought about that."

Right in the middle of the park, where the animals lived, was a huge lake. The zoo keeper had planned to row out in his boat and set off the fireworks on a tiny island in the middle.

"Good idea!" said the bigger animals cheering up no end.

So that evening when it grew dark, all the animals in the zoo watched a wonderful firework display as they stood safely on the shore of the lake.

6 The Noisy Toy Drummer

One day a new toy was put into the toy box with the rest of the toys.

It was a little drummer boy in a smart uniform with lots of gold braid and shiny gold buttons. "I've just been fitted with a new battery," said the little drummer boy, "so I shall be able to play the drum for hours and hours!"

All that day and most of the night, he played loudly on his drum. The other toys were rather cross, because they were tired and wanted to go to sleep.

"Please stop that noise!" some of the toys begged.

"I'm afraid I can't until my battery runs out," smiled the little drummer boy and carried on beating his drum.

All of a sudden some of the toys had a bright idea. They found two small corks and pushed them onto the ends of the drumsticks.

The little drummer boy kept on drumming, but at least it was quiet!

Now the tired toys can get some sleep.

7 Bath Time Toys

Andrew had lots of bath time toys. They floated in the bath water and bobbed about all around him.

"I wish I could stop them floating round the back of me," said Andrew. "I like to see all my toys!"

So, the next time Andrew's mother was out shopping, she bought a soap rack that fitted on the bath. Now instead of putting soap and sponges on it, Andrew keeps his toys there.

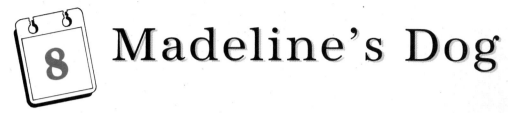

8 Madeline's Dog

Madeline's parents gave her a little dog for her birthday.

"What's his name?" Madeline asked.

"He hasn't got one!" her dad replied.

"You can choose his name," smiled Mother.

Madeline spent all that day and most of the next trying to think of a name.

"I want one that really suits you," she said hugging her little dog tightly.

That afternoon Madeline's little dog went into the backyard to explore. He found a heap of coal and sniffed around it until he was covered with dusty black marks.

When Madeline saw him she laughed out loud. "I'll call you Smudge, that suits you perfectly!"

9 Sing Along!

Everyone in the valley was looking forward to a grand concert in the village hall.

"The piano has fallen to bits!" sighed Ma and Pa Bramley. "Does anybody have a spare one?"

"We do," said the farmer and his wife, "but it's far too heavy for us to lift!"

"Send for Tessa and her breakdown truck!" shouted all the farm animals.

So Tessa rushed over to the farm, loaded the piano onto her truck, and Ma Bramley played all the way to the village while Pa and the others sang along!

10 Dressing Up

The weather outside was very bad and everyone had to stay indoors.

"Let's get the dressing up box out," suggested one of the children, "then we can have some fun!"

So the two children dragged the box from under the stairs and tried to open the lid.

"It's locked!" said the eldest boy. "Everybody look for the key!"

The children searched for ages, but no-one could find the missing key. They were very disappointed, but it wasn't very long before one of them thought of a good idea.

"We'll dress up in anything we can find around the house. Everyone has five minutes to find something!"

You'd be amazed what the children came back with. When their mother saw them, she laughed out loud and ran off to find her camera.

11 Belinda's New Apron

Belinda the ragdoll bought an apron with lots of roomy pockets.

"Is it to keep you clean when you do the housework?" asked her friends.

"Certainly not!" snapped Belinda who hated housework.

"Perhaps it's a garden apron and the pockets are for all your tools."

"Indeed it is not!" shouted Belinda angrily. "I might get my hands dirty if I worked in the garden, and that would never do!"

When, at last, Belinda put on her apron, she filled the pockets with all her favourite things. "Now I can reach everything I want very easily," smiled Belinda.

12 What Big Ears You've Got!

"Wouldn't it be fun," said Pete the pelican, "if we both went to tonight's party wearing false noses."

His friend, Ted the toucan, screeched with laughter. "Can we wear false ears instead? Our beaks are far too big."

"You're right!" laughed Peter. "We'll wear false ears instead!"

13 Harvey The Horse

Harvey the heavy horse was rather vain. The farmer often took him to shows and Harvey won lots of silver cups and rosettes, which he kept on shelves in his stable.

A few days before the Grand Heavy Horse Show, Harvey asked the farmer if he would buy him a special present.

"Depends what it is!" frowned the farmer. "It mustn't cost too much!"

"I would like a big mirror," said Harvey, quite determined, "then I could make sure that I looked just perfect before I went to a show."

So the farmer bought Harvey a mirror, which made all the other farm animals giggle when they saw Harvey admiring himself.

You're so vain Harvey!

14 Tessa Takes Harvey

On the day of the Grand Heavy Horse Show, the farmer was up very early getting Harvey ready.

But when it came to go, Harvey refused to move one single step.

"I'm not walking to the show, I shall get hot and tired and very dusty!" Harvey moaned.

The farmer shook his head. Then all of a sudden Tessa from the garage drove into the farmyard in her breakdown truck.

"Get Harvey aboard," she cried. "I'll drive him to the show on the back of my truck, then he'll be sure to win first prize."

And he did!

15 New Hot-water Bottles

The weather was turning cold. "I must go out and buy new hot-water bottles to keep you warm in bed this winter," said Mrs. Grey Rabbit to her children.

"Can we choose them ourselves?" cried the little rabbits.

"All hot-water bottles look very much the same," said their mother, "but off you go and bring back the ones you like."

Soon the little grey rabbits came home with a new hot-water bottle each. They look very different, don't they?

Claude Goes Jogging

One cold frosty morning, Clumsy Claude went jogging in the woods. As he thundered along, he bumped into every tree he came to.

"Whoops!" cried Claude. I'm so clumsy, I seem to have broken a few branches!"

But when Claude looked back, he got such a shock. "Whatever shall I do?" Claude gasped. "I've knocked down half the forest!"

Just at that moment up came Buzz the beaver with his chain saw.

"Don't look so worried," said Buzz. "I'll saw the fallen trees into logs, then the woodland folk can have warm fires this winter." And he started straight away.

"Next spring," Buzz told Clumsy Claude, "you can help me plant young trees, in place of the ones you knocked down!"

Elvis Builds An Igloo

Elvis the Eskimo went camping on the ice. He built himself an igloo from blocks of frozen snow.

He stayed in his igloo for a few days, but now it was time to move on.

I think there is somebody waiting to move in as soon as Elvis the Eskimo's back is turned.

The Pencil's Picture

18

Mark hadn't used his coloured pencils for ages. They were fed up with being left inside the pencil case.

"Let's jump out and draw a picture," suggested the black pencil. "I'll draw the outline and the coloured pencils can fill it in!"

"I'll colour the train," said the red pencil.

"I'll colour the sky," cried the blue one.

"I'll colour the grass and trees," the green pencil went on.

"Don't leave me out!" yelled the little yellow pencil.

"You can colour the sun," said the pencils all together, "then our picture will be perfect!"

I Can't Sleep

19

When night came and it grew dark, the Shy Little Kangaroo would say, "I can't sleep!" Then he would go and find his friend Wesley Wombat.

Now Koala couldn't sleep without his friend Wesley Wombat.

Would you believe it? Wesley Wombat couldn't sleep without his friend the cockatoo.

Then the cockatoo said "I can't sleep without my friend the Shy Little Kangaroo!"

So at last all the friends were together, everyone was happy and they all fell fast asleep!

20 Willy And The Duck

Willy the worm poked his head through the soil, and there standing right in front of him was a pair of webbed feet.

"A fat juicy worm!" quacked the duck. "Just perfect for my dinner!"

"What lovely webbed feet you have," said Willy shaking with fright. "Can you swim?"

"I can swim and I can fly," the duck went on. "In fact, I'm brilliant at flying!"

"I'd love to see a duck that can fly so well," said Willy, still shaking.

"Watch me!" cried the duck as she took off high into the air.

But Willy didn't stay around to watch, he wriggled back down his worm hole and never came out for a whole week!

21 Cheese Please!

Every mouse in the house felt like a change.

"I would like to live by the sea!" said one.

"I would love to live in a caravan!" said another.

"Let's live in a windmill!" squeaked the tiniest mouse.

"Somewhere safe, with lots of food and plenty of room for everyone!" suggested one of the oldest mice.

"Then I've found just the thing!" said Monty, who had been looking for ages. He led all the mice through a secret tunnel into the grocer's shop next door.

"Welcome to your new home!" giggled Monty as he pointed to an enormous yellow cheese. "There's lots of room and plenty to eat for everyone!"

22 Food Fight!

Two little hot dogs were feeling rather bored. One picked up the ketchup and the other picked up the mustard.

When the hamburgers saw what was happening they rushed across to join in the fun.

I wonder who is going to wash the tablecloth?

23 Lucille's Hats

It was a cold and frosty morning. "Just perfect for trying out my new hats," said Lucille the lop-eared rabbit as she looked out of her window.

Now in cold weather Lucille has a problem. Her ears are so long she can't get a hat to fit.

So she has sewed three hats together and now her ears will keep warm and cosy all through the winter.

24 Rolo's Cold

"At least I don't have to to put on my false red nose tonight!" laughed Rolo as he ran into the ring to entertain the children.

Rolo the clown had a dreadful cold. He had been snuffling and sneezing all day long.

"I hope you will be able to perform in the circus ring tonight," said the ringmaster looking rather worried. "If you don't, the children in the audience will be very disappointed."

"The show must go on!" sniffed Rolo, tucking a big box of paper tissues into the pocket of his baggy coat.

25 The Chipmunks' Thanksgiving

The chipmunks always looked forward to Thanksgiving. One of them cooked the food and the other told the story of the Pilgrim Fathers...How they crossed the Atlantic to America in the tiny sailing boat the 'Mayflower'!

...The first winter was very hard, but when at last spring came, they planted lots of seeds. Also a kind Indian named Squanto showed them where to find fish and how to trap turkey and deer.

By that autumn they had so much food to spare that they gave a party and invited all their Indian friends.

...And that very first Thanksgiving lasted three whole days!

26 Lost In The Fog

It was very foggy and everyone on Big Bear Mountain kept getting lost.

"This fog is going to last for a whole week," said one of the bears. "We shall have to take extra care when we walk up and down the mountain!"

"I know the answer," said one of the mountain rescue bears. "We'll travel roped together, that way no-one will get lost in the fog!"

27 Make It Snow!

Suzy and Harry were patiently waiting for the snow to come. They looked up into the winter sky and wished very hard, but it didn't snow, not even one tiny flake!

Grandma felt quite sorry for them. So, from a box in her attic, she took something she loved to play with when she was a child.

"This is for you both," she smiled as she gave the children a beautiful snow scene. "Now you can make it snow whenever you like - just by giving it a little shake!"

28 The Mail Train

"I'm rather worried," said Messenger Mole to his friend Mr. Grey Badger one morning in late November.

"Can I help?" asked Badger kindly.

"I shouldn't think so," sighed Messenger Mole. "Christmas is coming and soon all the woodland folk will be sending lots of mail. I don't think I shall be able to carry all the heavy parcels and bags of cards through the underground tunnels."

"Leave it to me!" said Badger, who was very good at solving problems.

A few days later he asked Mole to call at his house. And there parked outside, was Messenger Mole's very own mail train.

"It's marvellous!" gasped the excited Mole.

"It is rather good," grinned Mr. Grey Badger, "even if I do say so myself!"

29 Everyone Comes To Tea

It was a cold, damp, foggy day and the little grey rabbits were feeling glum. "Can we have some friends to tea?" asked one of them.

"Of course!" said Mrs. Grey Rabbit, who loved having visitors. "I'll get the food ready while you run off and invite a few friends."

So the little grey rabbits went into the woods and invited everyone they met.

When tea time arrived, the house was full of visitors. Mrs. Grey Rabbit had nowhere near enough chairs, and her table was far far too small - so all the little grey rabbits and their woodland guests sat up the stairs where there was plenty of room for everybody!

30 A Job For Gordon

"It's not long now until Christmas," said Gordon the gorilla. "I shall open my money box and find out how much I have to spend on presents."

But, dear, oh dear! When Gordon looked inside, he found nothing at all. His money box was completely empty!

"I must get a job," said Gordon, "then I will earn lots of money to buy presents for all my friends."

So straight away Gordon set off to find a job. He went into the biggest store in town and got one immediately.

"No-one will ever recognise me in this outfit!" smiled Gordon as he looked at himself in the mirror.

I think some of the children might, don't you?

DECEMBER

1

Julie's Advent Calendar

Julie was delighted, her uncle had sent her an advent calendar. The postman delivered it on the first day of December.

"Isn't it exciting?" cried Julie as she opened the envelope, "Christmas will soon be here!"

Julie saw that the calendar had twenty four tiny doors, one for each day up to Christmas Day. So she sat down and opened every one. Behind each door was a little picture and Julie looked at them all.

"Oh dear!" said her mother when she saw what Julie had done. "You're supposed to open one door each day until the last door is open!"

"Never mind," smiled Julie. "I'll close all the doors and begin again tomorrow!"

2

Sensible Slippers

Every year just before Christmas, Aunt Eve bought the children sensible slippers. They never looked scruffy and they never wore out - because they were so sensible.

This year Aunt Eve has given the children some money so they can choose their own.

Somehow I don't think they will have sensible slippers this year!

A Costume For Alice

3

Alice had an invitation to a party. "Not another one!" said her mother. "I do hope it's not fancy dress. I'm afraid I'm running out of ideas."

Alice looked at her invitation again, and at the very bottom printed in tiny letters it said *Come In Fancy Dress*.

The little girl sat down on the kitchen stool with her favourite doll in her arms. "I'll have to think of something," she told her mother.

"No need!" said her mother as she reached for Alice's doll. "I'll make you a costume exactly like your doll, and you can go as a Dutch girl!"

Sydney Is Different

4

Chrissy, Sissy and Missy were sisters. The three little penguins played all day long on an iceberg that floated in the cold water of the Atlantic Ocean.

"Aren't you three alike!" called the other creatures as they passed by.

"All penguins look alike!" cried a voice from the other side of the iceberg.

It was Sydney, the brother of Chrissy, Sissy and Missy.

"Everyone thinks I'm a girl," moaned Sydney, "and it's time I did something about it!" and he dived off the iceberg and swam away in disgust.

Before very long he was back. "Now everyone can tell the difference!" he cried as he showed off his brand new coat to Chrissy, Sissy and Missy.

5 The Twins Dress Up

On the last day of term, before school closed for the holidays, everybody joined in a fancy dress party.

"We want to look different," said the twins. "We are so alike that no-one can tell us apart!"

"Right!" said their mother. "You can both choose your own costumes. Gary can go to the costume shop in the morning and Lee can fetch his in the afternoon." So that was settled!

The afternoon of the party arrived and it was time for the twins to get ready. Gary took his costume from the box and so did his brother, "They're exactly the same," they cried together, "we're both going as pirates!"

"Too late to change now," said mother. "Gary you can wear your pirate's patch over your left eye, and Lee can wear his over his right. At last you'll look different!"

6 Bobby Robin's First Christmas

It was Bobby Robin's first Christmas, and he felt very excited. "Christmas is here! Merry Christmas everyone!" he chirped as he fluttered through the wood.

"It isn't here for at least two weeks!" twittered a passing wren.

"Then why do I keep getting presents of tiny white envelopes in the post every morning?" asked Bobby Robin rather puzzled.

"Those are Christmas cards!" laughed the other birds. "Open them and you will see!"

So Bobby Robin flew back home and opened his mail, and do you know, every one of his friends had sent cards with pictures of robins on the front!

7 Jonathon's Prize

Jonathon James Williamson was learning to write his name.

"With such a long name," smiled his teacher, "you'll have to practise extra hard!"

So Jonathan tried very hard indeed. He sat down with a very long piece of paper and wrote out Jonathan James Williamson over one hundred times.

Now one day, just before the Christmas holiday, the teacher asked all the children to write down their full name and put them all together in a big box. Then the teacher gave the box a good shake and pulled out a name.

"Jonathan James Williamson," she called out. "You are our lucky prize winner! You have won our school Christmas tree!"

So when school closed for the holiday, Jonathan took the tree home and the whole family thought he was great!

8 Who's Hiding?

When the snow is thick on the ground, everyone has to wear boots and remember to take them off at the kitchen door - then no-one leaves dirty footprints on the clean floor.

But you must always remember to check that your boots are quite empty before you put them back on again.

Empty boots make a great hiding place and you could be in for a big surprise!

9 The Fancy Hats

Fancy hats are fun! If you go to a party at holiday time, you almost always wear a fancy hat!

But how about choosing a fancy party hat for Moose?

It's impossible. There isn't one big enough! But don't worry Moose, the problem is soon solved - you'll have to wear lots of them!

Charlie Goes To A Party

10

It was Charlie's first party.

"You'll love it," said Charlie's young owner, "but you must not eat any trifle or chocolate or sticky cakes, because you are a puppy and rich food will make you sick. I've brought some tasty dog biscuits," smiled Charlie's owner, "they contain calcium and charcoal and marrow bone!"

"That sounds nice - I don't think!" Charlie grumbled as he disappeared under the party table.

Very soon the children gathered round and began to eat. Charlie sniffed the boys' shoes and licked the girls' ankles, which made them squeal and wriggle about on their chairs.

As the party went on, little tasty bits of food began to drop onto the floor. First a biscuit, then a ham sandwich. Charlie eagerly gobbled everything up...Next came a sausage roll, a few crisps, a chocolate marshmallow, then a whole fairy cake with pink icing on the top. Charlie really enjoyed that and ate it in one gulp - paper and all!

The children left the table and the party went on, but poor Charlie began to feel a bit sick.

At last it was time to go home, Charlie's owner picked him up and popped him inside his jacket.

"You have been a good dog," said the little boy on the way home. "With all the excitement I forgot to give you your tea, you must be feeling very hungry!"

But poor Charlie didn't feel hungry for a very long time.

What Went Pop?

11

Next day Charlie was feeling a lot better. He sniffed around his owner's bedroom and found a lucky bag brought home from the party. It was stuffed full of sweets and brightly coloured lollipops.

"I think I'll leave them alone," thought Charlie, then something else caught his eye. "Is it another puppy?" he woofed and Charlie bounded across the room to find out.

"You look like a puppy, but you don't smell like one or feel like one, and your far too quiet!"

All of a sudden there was a loud POP, and Charlie's new friend disappeared.

'I don't think I'll go to any more parties!' thought Charlie, and he went off to find some dinner.

The Reindeer Race

12

"Christmas will be here soon," called Santa Claus to his herd of reindeer as he strode through the forest. "I'll need some of you to pull my sleigh!"

Straight away some of them danced forward. "We are the strongest and fastest reindeer in the world!" they boasted tossing their antlers with pride.

As Santa Claus watched, they sped through the pine trees, heads held high.

"Watch out!" yelled Santa. But it was too late. The first reindeer bumped into a pine tree, then the next, and soon all the reindeer were in a tangled heap in the snow.

How Santa laughed. "There's no harm done," he grunted as he rubbed a reindeer's nose. "You may be the strongest and the fastest, but you'll have to learn to steer and stop before I'll let you pull my sleigh!"

The Snowmen's Christmas Tree

13

So much snow had fall during the night that the next morning the Garland children could make lots of snowmen, in fact they made snowmen, snowwomen, snowchildren and a snowdog - they even made a snowcat !

They built them round a fir tree in the middle of the lawn.

"They look like a real family," laughed one of the Garland children. "Let's decorate the fir tree, then our snow family will have a Christmas tree of their very own!"

On the branches, the children hung wreaths of dried apple, popcorn garlands and coconut shells, strings of marshmallows and stale bread shapes.

"It's a Christmas treat for the birds!" laughed one of the little children.

When darkness fell and everyone was fast asleep, I wonder if the snow family had treats from the tree too?

14 Special Delivery

It was Josh's job to deliver the Christmas gifts to friends all over town. This year there seemed more than ever and the boxes were definitely bigger than last year. Snow was falling and the paths were icy and very slippery.

"Have you any bright ideas?" Josh asked his dog Sandy as he opened the front door.

Straight away, Sandy bounded over to the garage, looked up into the roof and began to bark. Hanging high in the rafters was Josh's old sledge.

"Come on Sandy!" yelled Josh. "We'll have these presents delivered in no time at all!"

15 Baby Sister's Snowman

Josh made his baby sister a snowman, it was the first she had ever seen. She clapped her hands in delight and gurgled and laughed at her snowman all afternoon.

Now when it was time to come indoors and leave the snowman, baby sister screamed and screamed, in fact she screamed all through tea and most of the evening until at last she fell asleep.

"She liked her snowman so much," said Josh, "she wants one of her very own."

"You're right," said Mother. "I'll knit her one straight away, then we can all get some peace!"

16 The Bad-tempered Angel

Once upon a time, there was a beautiful Christmas tree. Its branches were decorated with sparkling coloured ornaments, lots of tinsel, chocolate decorations, pink sugar pigs and white icing mice.

Right at the very top was an angel doll with a very bad temper. "Wait until they light the candles on Christmas Eve!" she snapped. "All the chocolates and you silly sugar pigs and ice mice will melt!" Then she laughed.

But no-one need have worried. For when the candles were lit on Christmas Eve, nothing melted!

You see, the candles were electric and perfectly safe. They shone their lights brightly on the chocolates and the pink pigs and the iced mice, but they left the bad-tempered angel alone in the dark!

17 The Christmas Animals

Last Christmas Jamie was given a toy farm. It became his favourite toy.

"You've played with your animals a whole year!" said his mother. "Don't you ever get tired of your farm?"

"Not a bit," Jamie replied. "I love my farm, and this Christmas I'm going to hang some of the animals on the tree for a very special reason."

So Jamie chose the animals he thought might have been in the stable on the night that Jesus was born. Then he hung them on his tree to remind everyone what Christmas was really about.

18 The Angel On The Tree

"It's almost Christmas," Maria told her mother. "It's time to trim our tree."

So she took the decorations out of their box carefully one by one. But what had happened to the angel that stood on the very top? Sad to say it had fallen to bits!

"It's very old," said her mother as she held the pieces in her hand. "We'll have to make another!"

"How about a clothes peg doll?" laughed Maria. "We could dress her as an angel and she will crown our Christmas tree!"

19 A Shock For Dottie

Dottie Dormouse climbed up the branches of the Christmas tree. She nibbled a rich chocolate truffle and bit into a spicy gingerbread man.

'Yum yum!' she thought to herself. All of a sudden she let out a piercing shriek. "There's an enormous great mouse staring right at me, and she's wearing my best dress!"

Teddy's Christmas Outfit

20

Aunt Ruby made Lucy's teddy a brand new outfit for Christmas. Lucy tried hard to guess what it would be.

"Perhaps it's a scarf or a new pair of dungarees, or maybe a red tartan waistcoat!"

Now the next time Lucy saw her teddy, she was thrilled, for Aunt Ruby had dressed him up as Santa Claus with a little sack full of tiny gifts.

The Model Reindeer

21

One day just before Christmas, Santa opened a letter from a little boy who asked for a model reindeer.

Santa threw back his head and laughed. "I'm often asked for a model train or a boat, even an aeroplane, but never a model reindeer!" Then he looked on every shelf of his toy store, but could not find one anywhere!

So straight away he went to see his friend the woodcarver who had lots of model reindeer to choose from.

But when Santa pulled out the little boy's letter, he noticed that it continued on the back...*I would like a model reindeer big enough to ride on please.*

"Then I shall carve him one as quickly as I can," the woodcarver suggested.

The woodcarver finished just in time. At Christmas Santa Claus delivered the toy and the little boy who wrote the letter was delighted.

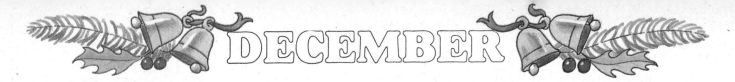

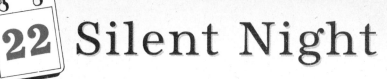

22 Silent Night

This beautiful carol is sung all over world around Christmas time. Young and old love 'Silent Night' whether it is performed in a cathedral or sung round the fireside at home.

It was all because of a family of greedy mice that this carol was written. A few days before Christmas, in a small town in the Austrian Tyrol, the parish priest had been to a house to welcome and bless a new born baby.

As he walked home in the dark, he looked up at the starry sky and wondered if Jesus might have been born on such a silent night. As he walked through the snow he wrote the poem we call 'Silent Night'.

On the day before Christmas Eve, the parish priest discovered that a family of mice had chewed their way through the bellows on the church organ. So at Mass on Christmas Eve, there would be no music and no singing!

Then the parish priest had an idea. He showed his poem to the choirmaster who wrote some music to go with the words in less than an hour.

On Christmas Eve the carol was sung in the little church, and because there was no organ, the parish priest played his guitar.

Everyone loved 'Silent Night' so much that in a few years it became the favourite carol sung at Christmas all over Europe and later the whole world!

23 Mrs. Claus Bakes Some Cakes

It was almost Christmas Eve and Santa and his helpers were filling sacks and loading up the sleigh for the next day.

Mrs. Claus was just as busy, she was baking and making lots of special treats for Santa to eat on his long journey across the sky.

"I can't take all that!" he gasped as he gazed at the food in her kitchen. "Have you forgotten that children all over the world leave me a little snack when I visit their houses. I'll soon be too fat to climb down the chimneys!"

So when Santa set off on the first stage of his journey, Mrs. Claus and all the helpers tucked into the delicious food she had made and wished one another a very Happy Christmas!

24 The Lost Present

Very late on Christmas Eve, Santa Claus and his reindeer arrived at the very last house to deliver presents.

As Santa reached into his sack, he realised that it was empty. He even turned it inside out and shook it hard.

"Oh my goodness!" gasped Santa sitting down with a bump. "I know I packed a present for every single child." He sighed as he took off one of his boots, for his feet were very tired.

Suddenly, Santa Claus roared with laughter, for there was the missing present. It had fallen down his wide-topped boot! So he crept down the chimney to deliver the very last present on his long list.

25

Santa's Spare Socks

"Does Santa Claus have any spare socks?" one of his youngest helpers asked Mrs. Claus.

"Go and look in the bedroom," replied Mrs. Claus rather puzzled, "and you'll find lots of clean pairs!"

It was Christmas morning when Santa Claus returned from his long trip across the world. He sat on the edge of his bed feeling very tired indeed.

As he gazed around the room he saw his clean socks hanging everywhere, and each one was filled with gifts from his helpers.

"How very kind," murmured Santa as he felt every sock. "I'll open them later!" And with that, he fell fast asleep.

26 Boxing Day Boxes

Santa Claus had kindly left all the children in the house presents they had wished for.

Everyone loved their gifts and spent the happiest of Christmas Days playing with their toys.

After the presents had been unwrapped, the children were very good and tidied up the paper. But the day after Christmas, the house was full of boxes of all different sizes!

"It's a shame to throw them away!" said the eldest boy.

"Let's play with them!" said another. "How about making something fantastic?" suggested one of the girls.

"I could hide inside," smiled the smallest child, "then you could try to find me!"

The boxes kept the children busy all that day. The grown-ups were not impressed.

"Next year," laughed their father, "you could simply ask for boxes and not bother with presents at all!"

27 Santa Steps On The Scales

Santa Claus had eaten so many snacks left out by so many children on Christmas Eve that his belt was far too tight.

"My dear!" he said to Mrs. Claus after Christmas, "I must go on a diet!"

Now some of his helpers overheard what Santa had said and decided to play a trick on him.

"You ought to get weighed!" suggested the cheekiest little helper. "I'll run and fetch the scales!"

So Santa took off his coat and boots and even his red trousers, then he stood on the scales.

"I can't possibly weigh as much at that!" he gasped as he watched the needle whirl round.

Poor Santa Claus! Perhaps he doesn't need to loose as much weight as he thinks!

28 Hare On Skis

Harold Hare was hopeless at skiing. His legs were too long and his big feet got in the way. He always ended up in a heap while the rest of his friends sped past him on their skis.

"I'm good at running and I'm good at football, and I'm very good at tennis!" Then Harold Hare stopped dead in his tracks. "That's the answer!" he cried, and ran indoors to find his tennis rackets!

Now Harold Hare is speeding over the snow as fast as everyone else!

29 The Teddies Make A Wish

"This year is coming to an end," said Teddy Grandpa. "We should be thinking of our New Year's Resolutions."

"Let's not make any," said Teddy Grandma. "Let's make a wish instead!"

Teddy Grandpa sighed. "I wish we had lots of little bears to visit us!"

"Some young visitors would be nice," agreed Teddy Grandma.

So there and then, she wrote on a large piece of paper: *Young Visitors Very Welcome. Please Call And See Teddy Grandpa And Teddy Grandma.*

They both went outside to pin it to the garden gate, but a gust of wind snatched the paper from Teddy Grandpa's hand and blew it high over the trees.

Poor Teddy Grandpa and Teddy Grandma went inside feeling rather sad and lonely.

30 A Wish Is Granted

Very, very early next morning there was a loud banging on Teddy Grandpa's and Teddy Grandma's back door. The bell at the front door was ringing too.

Teddy Grandpa and Teddy Grandma jumped out of bed and opened both doors.

"Your notice blew into our garden!" cried four of the smallest teddies you ever saw.

"Can we come in?"

"Tell us a story!"

"Will you take us fishing, and can we stay for breakfast?" they cried.

Teddy Grandpa and Teddy Grandma hugged all four little teddies with delight. "I think our wish has been granted!" smiled Teddy Grandpa.

31 Happy New Year

It was New Year's Eve and everyone in the wood had stayed awake very late.

The young mice had a shiny silver bell left over from Christmas and were looking forward to ringing in the New Year - but at one minute to midnight they found the tiniest mouse fast asleep inside the bell!

They needn't have worried for the bells of the church nearby rang out so loudly, they could be heard all over the wood.

And at midnight all the creatures wished each other a Happy New Year, except for the tiniest mouse who was still fast asleep in the silver bell!